INSIDE RUSSIAN POLITICS

INSIDE

RUSSIAN

POLITICS

EDWIN BACON

Biteback Publishing

As always, to Deborah, and to Eleanor,
Charlotte, Emily and Joanna.

First published in Great Britain in 2017 by
Biteback Publishing Ltd
Westminster Tower
3 Albert Embankment
London SE1 7SP
Copyright © Edwin Bacon 2017

ISBN 978-1-78590-231-4

10 9 8 7 6 5 4 3 2 1

A CIP catalogue record for this book is available from the British Library.

Set in Minion Pro

Printed and bound in Great Britain by
CPI Group (UK) Ltd, Croydon CR0 4YY

CONTENTS

CHAPTER ONE

GOING INSIDE RUSSIAN POLITICS

For anyone trying to understand the politics of Russia today, it can sometimes seem as if a wall has been built between us and our understanding of the world's biggest country. We want to gain insight into Russia and its politics but this wall is built of broad perceptions that obscure the detail and depth of field behind it. What we know about Russian politics is slap-bang in front of our faces: huge, unyielding, unpalatable facts – a mural of Putin, Crimea, Syria, Litvinenko, cybercrime and election meddling. There is the picture, there is the wall; what more do we need to know? A depressing number of politicians and observers seem happy to stop at the wall. Too often, particularly in British and American debates, Russia serves chiefly as a lens through which to view our own domestic politics, and the images of Russia in play tend towards the one-dimensional rather than the nuanced.

It is fair to assume, though, that those who have picked this book up want something more than the standard picture of Russia. They want instead to see over that wall and look inside Russian politics. There is, after all, plenty of depth and detail to be seen there – within, beyond and around the familiar story of an increasingly authoritarian Putin regime and its hazardous international adventurism. How did Russia's politics get to the state it is in today? Given the size and complexity of Russia, what are the limits on the ability of one man, Vladimir Putin, to govern? How are Russian politics arranged in terms of institutions and elections? What are the dominant ideas and divisive issues? Importantly, though too rarely considered relevant, what do Russia's people think about politics and the world today? What, too, about politics beyond 'the Moscow village', out there in a country so large that it spreads across eleven time zones? And how do we best conceptualise, shape and prepare for the Russia of tomorrow, knowing that new leadership and generational change are inexorably coming around the corner?

These questions and many others make up the content of this short book. It offers a counter-narrative of Russian politics, holding up to the light aspects of that country's political life too often absent from headline-driven stories. To be clear from the outset, though, this counter-narrative is not made up of some pro-Putin account that seeks to justify or obfuscate the policies of a regime marked, among other things, by venality, aggressive nationalism and the withholding of democracy. Nor, however, is it made up of a blindly pro-Western account that sees Russia in wholly antagonistic terms and brands as an apologist anyone who notes nuance, cites approvingly any policy or, indeed, seeks to explain Vladimir Putin's great popularity among the Russian people. The emphasis here is on understanding Russian politics and, while doing so, insisting that there is a difference between understanding and accepting or agreeing with it. As Andrew Monaghan – a British analyst of Russian affairs who has worked at both NATO and the Royal Institute of International Affairs – asserted in *The New Politics of Russia*, 'many in the West, particularly in political and media circles, so often get Russia wrong'; because of the way that they approach it, they see Russia as a country that defies logic.

'OTHERING' RUSSIA

If the analysis in this book has a single unifying theme that merits the term 'counter-narrative', it is that it rejects the 'othering' of Russia. It has no time for the idea that Russia somehow defies logic. In other words, the analysis here seeks to emphasise that neither Russia nor the Russians should be constructed in our minds or in our discourses as inexplicably 'other', a country and people whose actions and attitudes are too alien to ours to warrant considered analysis. Let us take just two specific examples of how this approach plays out in the chapters that follow.

In terms of public opinion, comparing the attitudes of Russians as a whole with those of Westerners reveals – for the most part – no great chasm between East and West. Not only, as might be expected, do the Russians share the same daily concerns about standards of living and their children's futures as do most people the world over, but when it comes to political attitudes not all is as a casual observer might assume. As Chapter Six explores, Russians are no more nationalist – perhaps even a little less so – than inhabitants of the United States and United Kingdom. They are also markedly less likely than the latter to think that an East–West nuclear conflict is heading our way anytime soon. Stemming to some extent from their geographically peripheral positions with regard to the European continent, Russia and the United Kingdom share a fundamental division in society that shapes important political decisions today: namely, the extent to which their country is a part of some concept called 'Europe' or not.

In terms of international relations, it might seem that differences in behaviour and approach between East and West stand at their most stark. Such a Cold War style dichotomy, however, not only limits perceptions of future policy options, but ignores the ebbs and flows of Russian foreign policy, even during the Putin era that began at this century's birth. As I elaborate in Chapter Eight, Russia has at times worked closely with the United States in its 'war on terror', including allowing a NATO transit hub for military personnel and supplies to operate in the southern Russian city – and birthplace of Lenin – Ulyanovsk, as recently as 2015. As alliances have been made and unmade and policy positions have shifted, it would be foolish to suppose that the international mood music has now simply stopped and that the foreign policies of different countries will sit in their current place from this moment on.

RUSSIA, WARS AND RUMOURS OF WAR

It is perhaps only natural that, for Western observers of Russia, international affairs are initially at the forefront of our concerns. At the time of writing in summer 2017, there are two significant wars in the world that involve Russia. One of these is taking place in the middle of Europe, in the Donbass region of Ukraine where more than 10,000 people have been killed in armed conflict since 2014 (see Chapter Eight). That conflict has received remarkably little coverage in the Western media, especially considering its European location, the scale of its casualties and the fact that 1.6 million people have been displaced as a result of the fighting. Coverage of the war in Syria, on the other hand, has been unrelenting. Officially speaking, Syria's President, Bashar al-Assad, has invited Russian forces into his country to assist in the quelling of uprisings on the part of the Free Syrian Army and various Islamist groups, including the Al-Nusra Front and the Islamic State (ISIS, also known as ISIL and Daesh). To this end, the Russian military is on the international stage in a way that has not been seen since the days of the Soviet Union, supplying air support, bombing rebel targets, and deploying and launching sea-based missiles.

The fact that Western powers, chiefly the United States, are also militarily engaged in Syria – and in a manner that suggests the prospect of direct US–Russian conflict – understandably heightens tensions and piques the interest of onlookers. The US military has given its support to the Free Syrian Army against President Assad, and has engaged in substantial military action against both ISIS and the Syrian military; in the latter case, notably launching a missile attack in April 2017 on the Shayrat Airbase having assessed that it had been used in the storage and delivery of chemical weapons. When, in June 2017, a US navy F18 Super Hornet fighter shot down a Syrian air force SU-22 fighter bomber, Moscow responded by halting its use of the incident prevention hotline with the United States – designed to avoid just the sort of occurrence that might escalate conflict – and declaring that US planes flying west of the Euphrates river would be tracked by Russian air defences as potential targets. It is military engagement of this nature that has played a part in moving the minute hand of the famous Doomsday Clock to two and a half minutes before midnight in 2017, its most pressing warning of imminent Armageddon since the early 1950s (see Chapter Nine).

Without wishing to unravel and assess the detailed complexities of the conflict, Putin's engagement in Syria demonstrates Russia's sense of itself on the international stage. Analysis of the Syrian war in isolation allows some conclusions to be drawn and positions to be taken, but a deeper understanding of Russia's position requires gaining an even greater perspective. In March 2014, when the US Secretary of State came out of six hours of negotiations with the Russian Foreign Minister in London, he perceptively alighted on the overarching factor influencing relations between Russia and the West in the present era. John Kerry's statement after the meeting emphasised its consideration of 'all of Russia's perceptions, their narrative, our narrative, our perceptions, and the differences between us'.

'Their narrative' amounts to far more than self-justification for Russia's actions in, say, Ukraine since 2014 or Syria since 2015. It is a sweeping narrative going back many years – more than 1,000 years in the case of President Putin's speech welcoming Crimea into the Russian Federation in March 2014 – that returns repeatedly to the collapse of the Soviet Union, the subsequent loss of Russian influence with regard both to contiguous countries and to the wider international order, including perceptions that the West, and particularly the United States, has taken unjust advantage of such weakness to the detriment of Russia in the decades following the demise of the USSR. Again, to identify this narrative is by no means to approve it. Acknowledging 'their narrative' simply represents a required level of understanding and a necessary, though insufficient, prerequisite for understanding Russia's foreign policy. In order to know a country and to get inside its politics, we need to know how that country sees itself. We might disagree with someone's political perspective, but we should take what they say seriously. To dismiss it is to treat them as something so distant from our normality as to be beyond our empathy. And in international affairs, particularly where nuclear-armed states are concerned, that is a dangerous position to take.

WHO PUT PUTIN IN?

So far, this chapter has dealt predominantly with Russia from an international perspective. Such an approach, however, represents a misleading guide as to what follows in most of this book, which focuses on the comparatively neglected area of Russia's domestic politics. If this book has one unifying theme – rejecting the 'othering' of Russia – it also has one overarching question that underlies our analysis of Russia's politics from chapter to chapter: how is it that the Putin regime rules Russia? It's a question intentionally designed to be taken two ways: firstly, why does the Putin regime rule Russia and, secondly, by what means does the Putin regime rule Russia? Let's take a look.

Why does the Putin regime rule Russia? When considering the politics of any state, it is always useful to start by asking why its leadership is the one in power. Think of it as though you are looking the powers that be in the eye and asking them, who put you in charge? Who gave you the right to make rules that you expect us to obey? You govern our economy and take money in taxes to spend on our behalf; what are you spending it on? You command the armed forces that are required for our country's security; are you making us more or less secure? These are difficult enough questions to ask of governments in established democracies where there is a pattern of and mechanism for throwing out rulers that get it wrong. These questions, therefore, are more difficult still in non-democratic countries such as Russia.

What is interesting in the case of Russia is that we know

what their answer is, but many observers – and possibly even the authorities themselves – don't believe it. Ask Vladimir Putin why he is the President of Russia and he would say it's because the people voted for him. And indeed, like most countries in the world today, Russia operates according to a democratic structure of government. When the Soviet Union collapsed in 1991, Communism departed the global political scene as an alternative system to liberal democracy across most of the world. Even Communism's most significant remaining adherent, the People's Republic of China, has moved away from its substance while retaining the label, seeming to prefer Confucius to Marx when it comes to the national awareness of its citizens. In the early 1990s, like all countries that emerged from under the rule of the Soviet Union, the Russian Federation adopted a democratic constitution. Drawing particularly on the US and French constitutions, it has all the political institutions that such a system requires: a directly elected President, a national parliament made up of two chambers –with the upper house representing the members of the Federation and the lower house being elected nationally – and acceptable term limits, initially of four years for both President and parliament, though that has now changed to six and five years respectively.

For several years, all of this was endorsed by Western governments. Indeed, I served as an accredited election observer in Russia's first post-Soviet general election in 1993 and was never in any doubt that the British delegation would confirm the democratic nature of the electoral process. But, as Chapter Two explores, more than a quarter of a century of Russian democracy has demonstrated a very basic flaw in the system that has taken some time to become apparent. That flaw is the failure of any Russian election to change the regime that rules Russia. Political scientists discuss democracy in great detail and the extent to which its definition should include not only systems and structures but also values and freedoms. Before we even get to that, though, democracy's most fundamental premise must surely be that the voters can throw a government out of power and usher in its opponents. Democracy is nothing unless those in power rule on behalf of and at the behest of the people. In Russia, each change of President – and there have been three since 1991 – has simply seen the incumbent's choice as successor take the role, along with accompanying promises and privileges for his predecessor.

Despite Russia's formal commitment to democracy, over the course of Russia's post-Soviet history we have seen the removal of any sense of fairness or surprise in a Russian election. The winning candidate does very little in the way of campaigning anymore, leaving that chore to those candidates who will lose. While it is easy to dismiss Russia's official democratic status as meaningless, the continued existence of democratic institutions in an otherwise undemocratic Russia matters – something I will go into greater detail about in Chapter Nine. Under its current regime, Russia's political system is one that seeks to show the attributes of electoral democracy without running the risk that those in power might actually lose an election. In short, Russia's democratic form does not so much bestow power as it is occupied by it.

DEEPER INSIDE RUSSIA

Russia's most recent parliamentary election in December 2016 operated under a system whereby half of the seats were allocated through a first past the post, constituency-based vote, and the other half by a proportional representation system based on a national party list. Unsurprisingly, Putin's party, United Russia, took more than three quarters of the seats in parliament. Its party-list vote was slightly less dominant, although United Russia still received an overall majority of 54 per cent on that half of the ballot. Among the most interesting of the nuanced analyses published after this election is a map produced by Russian analyst Alex Kireev that indicated Russia's political geography by considering who came second to United Russia across the country. Mostly the runners up across the country were one or other of the two 'in-system' opposition parties, the leftish Communist Party of the Russian Federation or the nationalist Liberal Democratic Party of Russia – except, however, for Moscow. In the dozen or so constituencies in the inner circle of Moscow, here, and only here, did second place go to the Western-style democrats from the party Yabloko. In Russia, as in Britain, clearly cosmopolitan capital dwellers are at political odds with the generally less well off, usually more nationalist, population of the country at large.

Inevitably, much of the focus of any look inside Russian

politics centres on Moscow and occasionally Vladimir Putin's home city and Russia's former capital, St Petersburg. Chapters Five to Seven of this book, however, look inside the institutional, popular and ideological heart of politics in 'majority Russia', where the writ of the Kremlin does not always run smoothly, and yet where Russia has repeatedly throughout its history retreated in times of peril. Since Vladimir Putin returned to the presidency for a third term in 2012, Russia's regime has taken a turn to a more authoritarian and nationalist style of ruling than it had in either of Putin's first two terms (2000–2008), and certainly more so than during the presidency of Dmitry Medvedev (2008–2012). Particularly since the annexation of Crimea in 2014, the regime's official discourse has moved decisively away from former talk of democracy and Russia's European destiny, and instead has heightened the sense that it is a nation whose security is under threat from the West. Such a threat is not always portrayed in military terms, but rather in a broader cultural sense, with Russian civilisation itself being in peril.

It is not an easy thing to define a civilisation, but broad ideas, symbols, pictures and impressions represent a helpful shortcut. At the risk of – and with due apologies for – caricature, what is Russian civilisation? In the eyes of newly fashionable but old-style ideologues emerging on the margins of the Putin regime in recent years, it is the vast steppe, wooden churches, elderly peasant women, onion domes, birch trees and, of course, Russian Orthodoxy. Moscow takes its place in such an amalgam, as do scientific progress and industrial production, but a retreat to Russian patriotism and towards greater economic self-sufficiency, spurred on by Western sanctions, has meant an increased focus on Russia beyond the capital. This suits Putin, since, as his conservative and authoritarian turn loses him support among the more liberal and globally connected populations of the big cities, he knows that such a stance plays well across much of Russia's vast expanse.

GOING INSIDE RUSSIAN POLITICS

No one should be surprised that when we look beyond immediate impressions and get inside Russian politics, there are complexities and nuances that deepen our understanding. While failings and malfeasances are common among leaders who seek power as a possession, rather than in the service and at the will of the people, straightforward governance could scarcely be the case in a nation with so rich a political history. Russia's shifting international allegiances, accompanied by resurgence in its military power projection, grab the headlines. Behind these leaders stands a political system that seems more stable and uniform than a closer inspection might support. Across Russia's different political groups and generations and regions, a variety of political views exist and are reflected in formal institutions, in the politics of the street and in discussions on blogs and around kitchen tables. Within and around the regime itself, disagreements about principles and approaches exist alongside competition for influence and riches. It is this deeper and more detailed understanding of Russian politics that this book seeks to reveal and analyse. It does so with an awareness that Russia is more than just Putin, and that we must not mistake today for forever.

CHAPTER TWO

HOW DID RUSSIA'S POLITICS GET LIKE THIS?

THE SHORT HISTORY OF RUSSIA'S DEMOCRACY

What was the point of Russia adopting a democratic constitution after the collapse of the Soviet Union? Did it change anything? As I said earlier, it is easy to look at Russian politics today and dismiss Russia's democratic choice in 1993 as meaningless. After all, one of the most succinct definitions of democracy is that it is a system where those in power lose elections. It's not enough for the people to have a vote. To be sure that democratic politics is embedded and works effectively, political leaders must be seen to accept that they hold power only on behalf of and at the behest of the people. A quarter of a century after Russia's democratic constitution came into force, however, the country has seen no change of regime at all.

There have been plenty of elections – to be precise, seven parliamentary elections and five presidential elections between 1993 and 2016 – but not one of them has thrown an incumbent regime out of office. One reason for this is institutional. Russia's constitution is about as presidential as it is possible to be – indeed, parliamentary elections in Russia cannot change the ruling regime – but it still just about remains within the democratic pale. Even when results weren't so tightly controlled, as was the case back in the mid-1990s, elections do not shift power. In 1993, the misnamed Liberal Democratic Party of Russia, led by the populist nationalist Vladimir Zhirinovsky, received almost a quarter – easily the largest proportion – of the popular vote in the party-list side of the ballot, but was granted not so much as a minor ministerial position. Indeed, in a presidential system, the governing executive is chosen by the President.

Surely, at least, the Russian President is chosen by the people? That's true enough, but in the short history of post-Soviet Russia the three Presidents have all represented regime continuity rather than regime change, since the triumphant presidential candidate put before the people was selected by the outgoing ruler. Russia's first post-Soviet President, Boris Yeltsin, was due to leave office at the end of his second term in June 2000, but, driven by his innate sense of the dramatic and the possibility of easing his preferred successor into office, Yeltsin resigned early and on live television on millennium eve, 31 December 1999. Yeltsin had chosen the relatively unknown figure of Vladimir Vladimirovich Putin to succeed him, and appointed him as Prime Minister in August 1999. According to the terms of the Russian

Constitution, should a presidential term be cut short, then the Prime Minister becomes the acting President and a new President must be elected within three months.

By resigning early, Yeltsin gave his preferred successor two invaluable advantages. First, the ruling regime had manipulated constitutional provisions so that the presidential election would take place in March 2000 and rival candidates, who lacked the presidential blessing, had been expecting and preparing for an election in June. Second, as acting President, Vladimir Putin stood for election with all the advantages of incumbency, such as a position from which to make popular decisions, the profile of power that proved so attractive to members of the Russian élite wavering over whom to support as Yeltsin's successor, guaranteed media coverage and an international platform denied to his rivals. British Prime Minister Tony Blair unwisely boosted Putin's international standing when, in March 2000, ignoring all norms about interfering in the elections of other countries, he and his wife made a high-profile visit to candidate Putin in St Petersburg a fortnight before the presidential vote. The UK government, along with the other major Western powers, was content to recognise Russia's presidential election of March 2000 as free and fair.

Russia's next change of President came in 2008, when Vladimir Putin was required to step down in line with the constitutional provision that a President can only serve two consecutive terms. Again his successor was hand-picked. Like Putin in 2000, Dmitry Medvedev, a long-standing protégé of Putin from his St Petersburg years, had never stood in an election before. Marked by President Putin as his successor, Medvedev was made First Deputy Prime Minister and given responsibility for the 'National Projects', a popular policy that involved spending money across Russia on health, education and infrastructure. With Putin's endorsement and a commitment to make his predecessor Prime Minister once he became President, Medvedev scarcely needed to campaign before being elected President in March 2008. Four years later, the process was reversed, and Putin was re-elected President in 2012 with the endorsement of the departing President Medvedev, whom he installed as his Prime Minister.

To return to our opening question then, what was the point of Russia becoming a constitutional democracy if the ruling regime has remained in power ever since? As we noted in Chapter One, the choice for democracy remains significant in today's Russia, even though the existing system is fundamentally flawed. The regime's commitment to a democratic constitution – note, not to a full and functioning democracy – has some substance in terms of legitimation and political discourse. The choice in favour of a Russia that is at least nominally and constitutionally committed to a democratic system of government has a shifting rationale and several key turning points.

TAKING A PATH MARKED DEMOCRACY

From the outset, the Russian democracy that was instrumental in pushing the already tottering Soviet regime over the abyss of history in 1991 was an amalgam of democratic and national-patriotic sensibilities. It was also the only realistic alternative on offer. Taking the democratic choice was more even than responding to the zeitgeist. It was an inevitability, a compulsion and an inexorable conclusion. This was Fukuyama's 'end of history' moment, when the Soviet collapse signalled the culmination of the bipolar global system and the introduction of what President Bush Sr called 'a new world order'. Liberal democracy was the way forward. Communism had turned out to be, as Vladimir Putin was to term it at the end of the decade, 'a cul-de-sac far away from the mainstream of civilisation'.

Yet, in this fusion of zeal for Russia's independence and the inexorability of a democratic path lay the seeds of the limitations of Russian democracy. The nationalism and patriotism that Boris Yeltsin employed as a rallying cry to the people as he sought their support and votes in opposition to Communism's authoritarian internationalism infected the yeast of democratic globalisation in Russia. When the economic collapse of the early post-Soviet years took hold, the concept of democracy came to be seen as an external imposition unsuited to Russia. As Vladimir Putin put it in his 'Millennium Manifesto' on becoming acting President in 1999:

> The experience of the '90s demonstrates vividly that merely experimenting with abstract models and schemes taken from foreign textbooks cannot assure that our country will achieve genuine renewal without any excessive costs.

The mechanical copying of other nations' experience will not guarantee success either. Every country, Russia included, has to search for its own path to renewal. We have not been very successful in this respect thus far. We have only started groping for our path and our model of transformation in the past year or two. Our future depends on combining the universal principles of the market economy and democracy with Russian realities.

How was it that the newly independent Russia's commitment to democracy as it is commonly understood in the West diminished so rapidly? In August 1991 Boris Yeltsin's then power-base, the Russian parliament, was threatened by tanks sent by members of the Soviet leadership organising a reactionary coup bent on turning back the tide of reform and restoring authoritarianism. Yeltsin had only recently been elected as President of a Russian Soviet Federative Socialist Republic, which at the time was still part of the Soviet Union and under the authority of Soviet President and Communist Party leader Mikhail Gorbachev. In a piece of political theatre that was both effective and heavy with symbolism, Yeltsin clambered onto a tank, shook hands with its crew and began to speak from scraps of notes held in his right hand, flapping in the breeze. In a determined tone, unaided by amplification, President Yeltsin denounced the old-style Communist coup plotters, asserting that democracy was 'acquiring an increasingly broad sweep and an irreversible character' in the country. Just two months earlier he had become the first elected leader of Russia in its history, winning a first round majority as almost 80 million people went to the polls. Less than a decade later, this same President Yeltsin was manipulating the electoral procedure and timetable in favour of his chosen successor, Vladimir Putin, who came to power bemoaning the infliction of democratic experiments based on foreign models and declaring that Russian realities must be taken into account.

There are multiple reasons for this drift away from early democratic fervour in Russia during the 1990s and awareness of them is essential if one is to understand how Russian politics has developed to its current state. The Putin regime identified itself from the start as a response to the 1990s. Its stated priority was the creation of stability and unity instead of the chaotic disarray that it associated – and not without reason – with the preceding decade. Why, then, did a full and functioning democratic system fail to establish itself in Russia during the years of the Yeltsin presidency? An explanation must begin with acknowledgement of the vast scale of the task being undertaken.

AN UNATTAINABLE DUAL TRANSITION

There is a body of literature in political science that concerns itself with democratic transition from authoritarianism to liberal democracy. As Communism collapsed between 1989 and 1991, Russia-watchers began to take this literature off the shelf and become familiar with it. At the same time, the 'transitologists' who had been its authors began to pay attention to the Soviet bloc, having previously been looking at democratic transitions in southern Europe and Latin America. The more astute scholars noted early on that Russia was no Spain or Portugal; indeed, Russia had no history at all of democracy. The nearest it had come was during the 'temporary government' of 1917 that had been swiftly swept from power by a Communist coup whose leaders summarily dissolved the parliament arising from Russia's first – and, up until the Soviet collapse, only – general election. Ever since 1917, the Russian and Soviet people had been propagandised and educated by a Soviet regime that was not only undemocratic in practice, but primarily defined itself as the superior system in opposition to the surely doomed liberal democracy of the exploitative capitalist world. The depth of anti-democratic inculcation in the Soviet bloc outdid anything that democratic transition theory had faced elsewhere.

What is more, the transition process about to be undertaken in Russia in the 1990s involved the transformation not only of political life, but also of the economy. This 'dual transition' again represented something new. When Franco had died in Spain, and when the military junta had moved off the political stage in Argentina, transition to democracy did not take place alongside the establishment of a completely new economic system. In the post-Soviet world, democratic transition arrived hand-in-hand with the introduction of a capitalist market economy to replace the 'command economy' controlled by the state. The impact in Russia was traumatic. Young reformers appointed by President Yeltsin,

faced with economic slowdown amidst the ideological con-
vulsions of the final abandonment of Marxism–Leninism,
moved to swiftly dismantle the Soviet economic system of
central planning and state ownership and to let the forces
of the market bring about a transformation. Transformation
certainly happened, though not in the way in which they had
intended. With price controls removed, hyperinflation put
basic goods out of reach and wiped out savings. With what
was left of the once powerful state revoking collective ownership of economic assets, kleptocratic 'robber capitalism'
strode onto the field of privatisation. It brought with it violence and corruption, as a few strongmen became fabulously
rich while most Russians experienced privation.

With economic collapse came a breakdown of the state's
social functions. Under the Soviet command system, where
state and industry were one, places of employment represented not simply the source of wages, but also provided all
sorts of social goods. These varied according to the nature
and location of the enterprise, but could include healthcare,
childcare, housing, leisure facilities, holidays and even con-
sumer services such as launderettes and hairdressers. As
the state divested itself, and therefore the Russian people, of
these assets, so its former provision of social goods became
the responsibility of the regional and municipal authorities.
At the same time, the fiscal system of the new Russian state
barely functioned. Junking a Soviet-style system in favour
of a rapid transition to a laissez-faire market approach left
significant legislative lacunae. Russia lacked the vast body of

company law and fiscal regulations that exists in states with established market economies – a situation that aided kleptocrats and hindered the collection of taxes by the state. As a result, the state did not have the resources to adequately perform its basic functions in terms of providing passable funding for hospitals, schools, the military, law and order and so on.

The dual transition represented a Herculean task. As Bill Clinton's campaign team sought to remind him during his successful 1992 presidential bid in the United States, elections are about 'the economy, stupid'. The idea that the Yeltsin regime could oversee economic collapse and the widespread impoverishment of Russia's population, while at the same time retaining popularity and receiving the votes of the people, represented a political conundrum. At the beginning of 1996, the election year, Yeltsin had an approval rating of around 3 per cent. In June, he polled over a third of the vote in the first round of the presidential election before going on to win the second round run-off against the Communist Party candidate, Gennady Zyuganov. Such a turnaround was managed partly by standard electioneering tactics. Yeltsin campaigned vigorously up to the first round before becoming seriously – though secretly – ill in the run-up to the second round. His campaign team developed a strategy of focusing the election around the question of whether Russia wanted a return to Communism or not; so stark a choice brought many reluctant Yeltsin voters on board. Between the first and the second rounds, the Yeltsin team gained the endorsement of Alexander Lebed, the military man turned politician who had finished in third place in the first round.

The Yeltsin campaign drew heavily on support from US political advisers, to a degree that would be unthinkable a couple of decades later when accusations of mutual meddling by the United States and Russia in each other's elections proves politically toxic. Much funding for the Yeltsin campaign came from Russia's newly minted oligarchs, who had joined the ranks of the global super-rich by profiting from the privatisation programme of previous years, and had no desire to see the patron of privatisation removed from his pedestal. Ever since Russia's pivotal election of 1996, opponents of the winner have sought to cast doubt on the results amidst allegations of electoral fraud.

DEMOCRACY NEEDS A DEMOCRATIC POLITICAL CULTURE

Although Yeltsin's election victory in 1996 contained elements of campaigning that are recognisable from democratic elections the world over, they did not point to Russia becoming a full and functioning democratic system. The 1996 presidential election had more in common with a plebiscite on Yeltsin than with an established electoral process. The President declined to identify himself with a political party, preferring instead to present himself as standing somehow above politics in the party sense. No Russian President has ever risen to his position through a political party. Instead, in the Russian form of democracy, political parties rise to prominence and power through the support of the President. By the mid-1990s, no effective party system had developed. The sequencing of the electoral cycle meant that parliamentary elections happened in the December of the year preceding the presidential election. In December 1995, Russia's voters entered their polling booths to be met with a ballot paper the size of a broadsheet newspaper, with the names and symbols of forty-three parties presented for them to choose from. The presidential nature of Russia's political system meant that there existed little motivation for ambitious politicians to hide their lights under the bushel of someone else's nascent political party, especially when they could better increase their personal profile by being the leader of their own party with all its attendant publicity, election broadcasts and possibilities for self-enrichment.

Russia's democratic development was held back, too, by the lack of a democratic political culture. The Soviet system had fostered unity rather than plurality, polarisation rather than compromise, denunciation rather than debate. Up until the reforms of the late Soviet years, to be a loyal citizen of the Soviet Union meant to support the Communist Party, while to oppose the Party was to be at best a dissident and at worst, an enemy of the people. There was little in the way of nuance in terms of the ubiquitous political education of Soviet citizens. Capitalism, bourgeois democracy, imperialism and the West which sheltered these evils – all these were the enemy and on the wrong side of history. When Soviet leader Nikita Khrushchev proclaimed 'We will bury you' to a group of Western envoys in 1956, he was not, as some have misinterpreted, threatening military action. He was re-stating the Soviet conviction that capitalism was inevitably dying and that the emergent and growing Communist world would be happy to oversee its funeral.

The politicians who came out of the late Soviet era on the side of reform and democracy had gained their political education in such a setting. They had lost any faith that they had in the Communist interpretation of the world, and had rejected that ideology in favour of a more Western-oriented democratic and capitalist worldview. But deeper cultural change is of a different order to a change in political conviction. There was a continuation among many in what might broadly be called the Yeltsin camp of a polarised political mind-set. From that perspective, democracy was not so much a political process or mode of behaviour involving give and take and the drawing together of multiple views, but was rather the label given to the winning side in the Soviet end-game. The democrats had won, and now they were in charge and could do what they wanted.

Boris Yeltsin himself had spent a decade as the Communist Party boss in the Sverdlovsk region, and had come to the democratic side late and with a populist bent. Critics argued that he had put on the cloak of democracy as an effective cover for his personal battle for power with Soviet leader Mikhail Gorbachev. Unsurprisingly, given his background, Yeltsin's actions were not those of a Western democrat. In August 1991, having successfully led the resistance to the coup against Gorbachev, he proceeded to humiliate the

Soviet leader on live television in front of the Russian parliament, handing him the minutes of a politburo meeting and brusquely commanding him to read them out loud. While Yeltsin towered over Gorbachev, wagging his finger at the diminished Soviet leader, there was much toe-curling on the part of democratic observers.

More significantly, Yeltsin's solution to the presidential–parliamentary impasse that arose in Russia in 1993 was – albeit eventually, after months of failed attempts to find a compromise – to send tanks to shell the parliament building, with over 100 of its defenders losing their lives. President and parliament had been at loggerheads over whether Russia's democracy should be a presidential system or a parliamentary one. Under the much amended Soviet-era constitution still extant in Russia in 1993, Yeltsin did not have the right to dissolve parliament, and parliament refused to dissolve itself. By October 1993, both President and parliament were prepared to use military force to settle the issue, and, once assured of the Russian army's support, Yeltsin did not hold back. In this manner, violent military action paved the way for the introduction of Russia's democratic constitution, and symbolised from the off the equivocal nature of its commitment to deep democratic values. Faced with very poor opinion polls at the beginning of 1996, members of Yeltsin's inner circle reportedly urged him to postpone what was in constitutional terms a compulsory presidential election. It is to his credit, and that of other members of his team, that he did not do so. Had he lost the election, whether he would have simply handed over the keys of the Kremlin to the leader of the Communist Party cannot be taken as a given, although it must remain a matter of counter-factual conjecture.

HALF-WAY TO DEMOCRACY

Having set out to answer the question of why a full and functioning democratic system failed to establish itself in Russia during the years of the Yeltsin presidency, we have identified a number of factors. In relation to democratic transition alone, the heavily presidential institutional arrangements that were enabled by the violent dissolution of Russia's parliament in 1993 served to stymie the development of a party-based system. The President appoints the Prime Minister and oversees the government. Parliament's role is limited, and so any struggle for power is focused on the executive rather than on the legislature. President Yeltsin, like his successors, preferred to keep his distance from political parties and, when he facilitated the establishment of a 'presidential party' for parliamentary purposes, the party was his creature rather than he being its.

In 1993's parliamentary election, the party Russia's Choice had been the President's favourite. Later dissatisfied with Russia's Choice, however, he approved the formation of and – somewhat at a distance – supported the party Our Home Is Russia in 1995's election. That election represented an unhelpful introduction to the notion of multi-party democracy for Russia's people, with forty-three parties on the ballot – the vast majority of which were unknown to and indistinguishable in the eyes of most voters. There is such a thing as too much choice, even in democratic politics. The results of the 1995 election did, however, go some way to firming up Russia's party system, since, with so many parties competing, only four were familiar enough to receive sufficient votes to qualify for parliamentary seats under the party list half of the ballot. Three of these four parties – the Communist Party of the Russian Federation, the Liberal Democratic Party of Russia and the Russian United Democratic Party (Yabloko) – continue to have a presence in Russian politics today. The remaining one of these four – Our Home Is Russia, the party closest to President Yeltsin – disappeared once President Putin came to office. As with his predecessor, Putin owed nothing of his rise to power to any political party and, once safely installed in the Kremlin, he preferred to bring his own party – United Russia – into existence.

Alongside these institutional barriers to democratic transition, we have also noted the difficulties involved in trying to rapidly change a country's political culture. Inevitably, those in a position to assume leadership in the immediate post-Soviet years were formed by the old political culture. In a number of other countries formerly part of the Soviet Union or the Soviet bloc that adopted democracy in the years 1989 to 1991, the process of rejecting Communism had also been one of rejecting what was seen as Russian occupation or dominance. Leaders emerged – for example, Lech Wałęsa in Poland and Václav Havel in Czechoslovakia – who had been formed by opposition to the ruling Communist regime, rather than by rising to prominence within it. Not so, however, in Russia and most of the former Soviet states. The crimes and failures of the Soviet regime were by no means hidden, but there was not a particularly vehement denunciation of all things Soviet. Yeltsin's political appeal was built on a rejection of the Communism that he had previously espoused. Putin has similarly criticised the excesses of the Soviet era. At the same time, though, there were no trials of those responsible and no lustration laws introduced. The failure to cleanse the political stables in this way meant a failure to address the dominant political culture. None of Russia's post-Soviet leaders and very few of their appointees have any experience of grassroots democratic politics. The first elections that both Vladimir Putin and Dmitry Medvedev took part in were for the position of head of state.

HALF-WAY TO MARKET

Having emphasised the institutional and cultural barriers to democratic transition in 1990s Russia, we then stressed the monumental difficulties posed by the attempt to complete democratic transition at the same time as establishing an entirely new economic system. Cultural difficulties came into play in this area, too. Just as the political leaders had no experience of democracy, so those who began to engage in business had no experience of a functioning market economy. Only a few years earlier, the very concept of profit came with negative connotations of exploitation and ran counter to both Soviet law and Soviet morality. Plenty of Soviet citizens engaged in the 'black market' or second economy, but this was at best frowned upon and done behind the backs of the authorities. Once profit and the market suddenly became not simply approved of and encouraged by what remained of the state, but also essential to keep food on the table, the old Soviet propaganda images of ruthless capitalists who exploited others for profit represented the only model that many knew. In addition, the weakness of the state and the lack of an appropriate legal infrastructure were a boon for the Russian criminal fraternity. The word 'business' had no real Russian equivalent and so was simply adopted, in transliterated form. In practice, much *biznes* sat close to that other adopted foreign word that came to the fore in the 1990s, *mafiya*.

The cultural clash with Western ideas went both ways, as Western governments sought to encourage those activities that might be construed as the early signs of democracy and the market economy. If it called itself democratisation or marketisation, then it was to be encouraged. British government policy towards Yeltsin's Russia in the 1990s sought to support, in the words of the Foreign and Commonwealth Office, 'political stability and democracy'. That there was a potential contradiction between these two goals received no acknowledgement. The criminal excesses of the Russian *mafiya* became seen, in the eyes of some, as the inevitable teething troubles in the emergence of law-abiding entrepreneurs, with parallels being drawn with Chicago in the 1920s. The English novelist Sophia Creswell, who lived in Russia during the 1990s, illustrates beautifully the naïveté of some

Westerners as they observed what was happening. English girl Natalie meets a thuggish, thick-set, skin-headed 'businessman' who is setting up a bank in the flat next door.

> Five years in the gulag and now I am a businessman. The camps are the best business schools in the world, you have to be hard. You will see, soon nobody will be able to beat Russian businessmen ... Banking, forestry, light metals, import and export, construction work. I will turn my hand to anything but you have to watch everyone. They are all crooks, everybody is a crook. They will steal your equipment, steal your grandmother. Everybody needs protection.' ... 'And what kind of bank will it be?' I asked in horror. 'International,' he said grandiosely. 'The International Bank of Friendship ... So, old-fashioned young English girl! Ha! What are you thinking of? Marble halls eh? This will be a private bank, just for friends. A fax, a telephone and a computer. (Sophia Creswell, *Sam Golod*, 1996)

By the mid-1990s, according to some estimates, there were around 3 million people in Russia working for mafia gangs. In the eyes of many Russians, *biznes* and *mafiya* were synonymous. Since the dual transition of democratisation and marketisation was the policy of the Yeltsin government, it is scarcely surprising that Russians merged the two together in their minds. In the minds of many at the time – and perhaps more since, given that the narrative of the Putin regime has repeatedly made this point – Western-style democracy meant decline.

During the 1990s in Russia, average life expectancy fell by about four years; though, from the mid-1990s onwards, the trend moved slowly upwards, albeit from a low starting point that, at one point, had average male life expectancy in Russia as low as fifty-eight years. There is evidence, such as that provided in the UK medical journal *The Lancet* in 2001, to argue that the fall in life expectancy had more to do with alcoholism than with poverty – though, of course, alcoholism and poverty are not unconnected. US scholars Andrei Shleifer and Daniel Treisman make the case that the economic decline in Russia during the 1990s was not as catastrophic as is commonly held, and that Russia was, and indeed is, a 'normal country' in terms of being much like we would expect a middle-income country to be. Nevertheless, the economic data that Shleifer and Treisman used (primarily related to consumption) are not all. The socio-economic dislocation of the Soviet collapse and subsequent dual transition process brought about unemployment, anxiety for the future, and a disruption of the fundamental certainties of everyday life. Such factors led to the shocking conclusion that, as the normally sober *Economist* magazine overstated, 'mass privatisation was mass murder' (22 January 2009).

To be clear, economic decline and a fall in life expectancy began towards the end of the Soviet years, and the blame ought not to be laid solely on the post-Soviet reforms. That said, the experience of the early 1990s in Russia took the inflated hopes of many already impoverished citizens about what democracy and the market might achieve, and dashed them with unusual force. This experience discredited democracy in the eyes of plenty of Russians, especially those of a certain age who had made their careers in the Soviet system and lacked the skills, energy and opportunities to make their lives anew. What is more, since Vladimir Putin became President in 2000 the chief narrative of his regime – repeated so often that it has become hegemonic – emphasises that the 1990s was a decade of poverty, chaos and national humiliation.

TRIPLE TRANSITION IN RUSSIA

Noting the institutional and cultural flaws in Russia's democratic transition, and adding the socio-economic catastrophe that made up an attempted dual transition, is perhaps enough to explain the failure of Russia to develop a full and functioning democracy. But one further decisive element demands identification if we are to more fully understand how Russian politics became the way it is today. What was attempted in 1990s Russia was not simply a democratic transition. Nor even does the term 'dual transition', creating a market economy at the same time as a democratic system, encapsulate it. Instead, Russia underwent a 'triple transition'.

The concept of the post-Soviet triple transition owes its genesis to the German scholar Claus Offe, who noted in 1991 that alongside questions of political institutions and economic resources, for post-Communist states 'at the most fundamental level a "decision" must be made as to who "we" are'. As well as establishing a new political arrangement and a new economic system, post-Soviet Russia faced the task of establishing a 'new' country. It is too often forgotten that geographically, politically and historically, Russia is not simply a continuation of the Soviet Union. Although Russia took on many of the obligations and privileges of the Soviet state, for example its debts and its status as a permanent member of the UN Security Council, it was also the chief perpetrator of the USSR's demise. The rise of Russia lay behind the fall of the Soviet Union. At his inauguration as the first democratically elected leader of Russia in July 1991, when Russia was still one of fifteen republics that made up the Soviet Union, Boris Yeltsin declared that 'Great Russia is rising from its knees'. Emphasis was laid on the idea that the mighty nation of Russia had been subsumed for more than seventy years under the Soviet state and was now re-emerging. The Russian parliament – the Duma – that was elected in 1993 was officially referred to as the Fifth Duma, with the previous four having sat under Tsar Nicholas II between 1906 and 1917. The discourse was of the evolutionary democratisation of the Russian Empire having been interrupted by the revolution of 1917 and the imposition of an authoritarian Communist regime that had now at long last been overthrown, allowing Russia to rejoin the democratic path it left seventy-five years earlier. As with the decisions made with regard to democratic transition and economic transition, the stance of the Yeltsin government on the third element of the triple transition – nation-building – set the framework for the Russian politics that we see today.

The idea of great Russia rising from its knees encapsulates so much that has driven the Russian politics of the Putin era. Talk of Vladimir Putin being a great admirer of the Soviet Union, or even of Stalin, is overblown and must be tempered by awareness of where he, his regime and the Russian state position themselves in historical terms. One of the major public holidays in the Soviet year was Revolution Day, 7 November, which marked the Communists' seizure of power in 1917 and was the national day of the Soviet Union. Under President Yeltsin, Revolution Day was downgraded and renamed the Day of National Reconciliation. It was not until the Putin era, though, that 7 November was removed completely from the list of officially recognised days in Russia, at the same time as National Unity Day, 4 November, was instituted. This new holiday commemorated Moscow's liberation from Polish invaders in 1612 to bring to an end the Time of Troubles and interference in Russia by powers to its west. President Putin has done more to associate himself with Russia's pre-Communist Imperial era than with the Soviet state. At his behest, the remains of General Denikin, who commanded the White forces against the Communist Reds in the Russian Civil War (1918–1921), were reburied with due ceremony in Moscow. Putin's Russia seeks a balance between respecting the achievements of the Soviet era, admiring its strength and standing in the world, but preferring straightforward Russian nationalist 'great power' status and influence to the ideological baggage of Soviet socialism and internationalism.

The results of the post-Soviet nation-building inherent in the process of triple transition play out in the renewed tensions between Russia and the West that brought relations to their lowest point since the Cold War in the years after the annexation of Crimea in 2014. The claim here is not that such a downturn was by any means inevitable. We explore elsewhere – in Chapter Eight principally – the particular steps that led to so serious a degradation in relations between Russia and the West, with all its accompanying security concerns and threats of military conflict. For now, though, two aspects of recent history merit a mention: specifically, the renewal of the centuries-old Russian debate over the extent to which it is a European power or a distinctively separate Slavic civilisation, and the related and consistent determination that post-Soviet Russia retains a decisive voice in global affairs.

RUSSIA'S HISTORY OF IDEAS IN TODAY'S POLITICS

To some, the idea might seem strange that Russian politics can still be moved and shaped by what many would consider arcane debates that go back to nineteenth-century philosophical discussions between Slavophiles and Westernisers. If you live in Britain, however, the almost elemental force of disputes over whether a country is European or not should seem a little less obscure. Although the Russian Constitution, in reaction to decades of Soviet rule, explicitly rules out the adoption of a state ideology, the Putin regime informally subscribes to a concoction of ideas bringing together the uniqueness of Russian civilisation, Russia's quasi-messianic mission to serve as an example to the rest of the world and an alternative to hegemonic Western ideas, a commitment to Russia's 'great power' status and influence, and a celebration of the innate qualities and achievements of the Russian people. As Chapter Seven sets out in more detail, the philosophers, authors, scientists and publicists who support this ideological framework come from different streams of thought – Orthodox, Communist and right-wing nationalist. Once again, the roots of the Putin years can be seen in the 1990s.

President Yeltsin was at least as much a national patriot as a democrat. Under his guidance, a national competition was launched to define the amorphous and elusive 'Russian idea', emphasising the 'otherness' of Russia in relation to the West, which always and increasingly served to bolster nascent inimicalness. When the transition to a market economy went badly, such an emphasis made it easier for critics to blame the West. Just as with Communism, it was the import of Western models unsuited to Russia that was the problem. Many in Russia cling to the generalised myth, demonstrable as such with even a cursory glance at the available data, that Russians are spiritual and able to share in contrast with materialistic and selfish Westerners. As relations between Russia and the West worsened, the discourse changed from the reasonable premise that the market reforms of the 1990s caused economic hardship, to a harder edged re-interpretation of recent history that had Western advisers deliberately undermining the Russian economy in order to weaken the Russian state. The idea gained traction that, as Vladimir Putin was to put it many years later, Western powers thought 'now that the Soviet Union has fallen apart, we need to finish Russia off'.

Self-perceived 'otherness' – for all its justification in terms of Russia's strategic, historical and geopolitical significance – drew a boundary around what was possible. When NATO established its Partnership for Peace programme as a first step to closer relations with the former Communist world, Russia would not countenance becoming just another of the states signing up to a Western programme. Russia insisted on a position apart and a special status was granted through a Russia–NATO Council. When the European Union drew up a series of bilateral agreements as part of its Eastern Neighbourhood programme, Russia did not warm to the idea of being counted in the category of a mere neighbour of the EU. It sees itself with some justification as more than that particular descriptor allows. When NATO took military action against Serbia at the end of the 1990s, Russia sided with its fellow Slavic nation and bridled at the ease, both diplomatic and military, with which NATO operated without much concern for Russian reaction.

ERASING THE MILLENNIUM LINE
It is too simple to draw a line between the Yeltsin and Putin years, and to see the latter alone as the site of a decline in Russia's democracy and in relations with the West. Yes, such

a decline took place, but neither as a *volte face* from what had gone before, nor in a straightforward linear process. When Putin first came to power in 2000, his foreign policy for a good few years involved improving relations with the West compared to their state at the end of the Yeltsin era. His first foreign visit as President of Russia was to London to meet his new friend Tony Blair – an honour bestowed perhaps partly as a reward for the British Prime Minister's exceptional election-meddling trip to St Petersburg a few weeks earlier. President Putin was also the first foreign leader to call President Bush after 9/11, when he offered assurance that Russia would make good on promises with regard to prosecuting the 'war on terror'.

Nor is it quite possible, as the narrative of the Putin regime would like it to be, to draw a line between the Yeltsin and Putin years in terms of economic growth. It is certainly the case that, on the back of a precipitous rise in energy prices, the Russian economy grew during Putin's first two terms (2000–2008). But that period of unbroken economic growth actually began under Yeltsin in 1999.

As this chapter has sought to illuminate, questionable democracy and a problematic relationship with the West were features of Russia's first post-Soviet decade and, in this sense, are not a Putin-ite departure. It is too simplistic to understand today's Russian politics as solely the malformed creation of one man and his regime. The institutional choices of the 1990s limped out of the crash between Russia and the Soviet Union. They created a system where the presidency is all, and thereby stymied deeper democratic development. The complexities of a triple transition demanded that decades of polarised authoritarian rule shift rapidly into liberal democratic mode, at the same time as transforming the socio-economic foundations of the state, at the same time as recreating Russian nationhood. None of which is to gainsay the assertion that Russia's leaders might have chosen, as much of this book explores, more enlightened policy paths. But awareness of what has gone before enhances our understanding of the choices made inside Russian politics.

CHAPTER THREE

RUSSIA'S RULING REGIME

THE PIKALYOVO INCIDENT

'It is absolutely unacceptable', Vladimir Putin declared with slow deliberation, glowering at those who sat around the plain wooden table in the small industrial town of Pikalyovo, a few hours' drive to the east of St Petersburg, in the early summer of 2009.

'Thousands of people are affected', he continued.

Casually dressed, Putin sat alone at the head of the table. He spoke slowly and angrily, looking directly at the assembled managers and bosses seated along the sides of the table either side of him. He blamed them for a failure to pay wages to workers in Pikalyovo and for the running down of the local factory. Drawn to the town by a series of demonstrations organised by the impoverished workforce, Putin addressed those assembled with the air of a head teacher simultaneously furious and disappointed after his trusted prefects had trashed a local pub. He attributed the demonstrations to the 'lack of professionalism, and sheer greed' of the company chiefs gathered before him.

Half-way down the table on Putin's left sat Russia's then richest man, Oleg Deripaska, who was looking down with his hands clasped in front of his face. A year earlier he had made headlines in the UK when newspapers detailed his meetings with senior Labour minister and EU trade commissioner Peter Mandelson, including one in Moscow's swanky Pushkin Café, and with then shadow Chancellor of the Exchequer George Osborne, on Deripaska's yacht in Corfu. In scruffy Pikalyovo, the billionaire, seated with many others around a plain table in a small shabby room, was shown on television as Vladimir Putin demanded that the executives sign an agreement to address the workers' complaints.

When they had signed it one by one, Putin picked up the document with a look of disdain, and looked directly at Deripaska.

'Oleg Vladimirovich, have you signed this?'

'Yes.'

'I can't see your signature. Sign it.'

Beckoning the billionaire with a wave of his hand, he commanded him,

'Come here.'

At which Russia's richest man, in front of those in the room and those watching on television, got to his feet, scraping his chair legs on the wooden floor, squeezed past his still seated employees, and made his way to the head of the table.

Putin gestured at the agreement on the table in front of

him. Obediently, Deripaska signed his name. He then turned to head back to his seat, only to be called to a halt.

'Give me back my pen', said Putin.

And the billionaire did just that before returning to his place.

A couple of minutes spent online watching a clip of that encounter between the billionaire oligarch and the then Prime Minister Putin provides a more forceful picture than several explanatory paragraphs of how politics inside Russia differs from that in Western liberal democracies possibly could. The Pikalyovo incident encapsulates a number of aspects of how Russia's politics works. It illustrates what many take to be the standard modus operandi of an authoritarian system with an unchallenged leader acting dictatorially. It shows the linkage between politics and the super-rich oligarchs as the élite sit together in a room to sort out between them what happens to the ordinary citizen. It demonstrates a tendency towards what has become known as 'manual control', where instead of systems functioning effectively to resolve issues, even relatively minor problems in terms of the national interest rely on the personal authority of Vladimir Putin for resolution. It reveals the gap between formal positions and informal authority, as someone who in formal terms was merely the number two in the state hierarchy (at that time Dmitry Medvedev was President and Putin his Prime Minister) interferes in a private business matter.

Hints are to be found concerning less well publicised – and, indeed, what we might call more normal – aspects of

Russian political life. A moment's thought is all it takes to realise that the world's biggest country cannot be run in this manner, with one man overseeing from Moscow the minutiae of life across eleven time zones. A considerable institutional structure of government ministries and civil servants at federal, regional and municipal level exists in Russia. In Pikalyovo itself, to implement Putin's solution required complex manoeuvrings and budgetary diversions in the short term and, several years later, with the Kremlin's attention elsewhere, the workers were subject to cutbacks and reductions in hours that once again impoverished them.

Pikalyovo is only unique because of the high-powered attention it received. The problem of declining single-industry towns remains widespread; it cannot be solved by an angry politician shouting at people on national television. Instead a careful programme is required, and it is in the less publicised and more detailed setting of Russia's government and associated policy centres that specialists work on such programmes. Russia's Ministry of Economic Development lists over 300 *monogoroda* (mono- or single-industry towns) and has carried out detailed analysis, dividing them into three risk categories in order to prioritise, and adopting a range of different policy approaches. These policies chiefly revolve around various methods of subsidy in order to maintain some viability and socio-economic stability, and to ameliorate over a prolonged period of time the economic and political difficulties posed.

The Pikalyovo incident was politics as theatre, such as

happens the world over – albeit with a particular Russian slant. So staged an event depicted Vladimir Putin as the benevolent leader displaying empathy for the common man and woman. It played to that broadest of constituencies that – despite what many assume – continues to be of vital importance to Russia's ruling regime: namely, ordinary Russian people. In terms of boosting regime popularity, the rather populist and simplistic piece of political theatre broadcast across Russia from a small room in Pikalyovo portrayed Putin as resolutely on the side of the impoverished working man and woman, standing up at last against the 'super-rich'. The effectiveness of its straightforward appeal is clear. After all, the sight of the wealthy brought low on behalf of the little man would play well the world over. In Russia it plays particularly well. This is a country whose Soviet-educated citizens imbibed the values of egalitarianism for years before the new post-Soviet Russia saw a tiny minority get very rich while most of the country lagged far behind. Today Russia has a markedly high level of wealth inequality; when it comes to the amount of wealth owned by a small group at the top, data from the annual Credit Suisse global wealth survey in 2016 put Russia out ahead in terms of global inequality, with 10 per cent of the population owning almost 90 per cent of the wealth, and three quarters of Russia's wealth being owned by 1 per cent of the population. For all his Pikalyovo posturing, Putin and his regime remain vulnerable to the charge that they facilitate and participate in such inequality and that corruption and the abuse of power go a long way to explain it (Chapter Four sets out the central place of corruption in Russia's opposition politics and Chapter Six demonstrates the regime's vulnerability on this issue when it comes to public opinion).

The message did not simply involve presenting to the people the picture of a regime that is on their side. It also involved reminding the oligarchs who the boss is. To those who might challenge the regime, particularly among the élite, it was an elemental display of power, indicating with brutal bluntness who is really in charge. The direct intervention of the Kremlin in the running of a company was accompanied by the threat that, in relation to the dispute at hand, if the owners did not come up to scratch and restart the factory then – as Putin asserted – 'one way or another, we will do it without you'. The implication seemed plain that if the super-rich did not do what the state demanded, then it would be done without them. This was a warning that applied not just to a small factory in a small Russian town, but to the state's ability to control business and wealth more widely.

RUSSIA AND NORMAL POLITICS

Discussion of Russian politics in the West understandably tends to concentrate on big names and issues of global significance. Pikalyovo was all about Mr Putin and, indeed, from the beginning of the twenty-first century for most interested observers of Russian politics, it's been all about Mr Putin and those issues that sit with his name in the scandalous headlines – the decline of democracy and human rights, corruption, spy scandals, murders and military conflict. In most countries, however, and Russia is no exception in this regard, what concerns the people most in the long run are the more prosaic matters of everyday life. After all the propaganda of nationalism, the annexation of Crimea and the ratcheting up – by both sides – of tension with the West, opinion polls in early 2016 by the respected polling agency Levada (see Chapter Six) indicated that, when asked to identify the single greatest threat to their country, the majority of Russians alighted on economic decline. This is normal, and not something to be interpreted through the prism of East–West relations. As with people the world over, Russians' hierarchy of needs places considerations of income and well-being ahead of more abstract notions such as national prestige. When pollsters *do* insist on bringing these two aspects together, around three quarters of Russia's population do not want to see their government climb down over Ukraine just for the sake of easing Western sanctions.

Let us not, however, fall into the interpretive trap of bringing such aspects together and seeing everything in Russia solely in relation to international tensions and the person of the President. The tendency for most considerations of Russia to concentrate on foreign affairs rather than on what happens inside Russian politics serves to provide only a partial understanding of that great country. Behind all the headlines and our perhaps inevitable preoccupation with Putin, the Russian government adopts and implements policies across the broad sweep of more run-of-the-mill but nonetheless essential areas common to any developed country. While there is some coverage in the West of Russian economic policies and prospects in general, we rarely – outside of the Russia-watching community – get to hear much about vital everyday questions such as healthcare, education, housing, infrastructure and so on. Yet, these are, of course, areas of vital concern for Russia's citizens, and considerable effort has been made during the Putin years to deliver. As noted in Chapter Two, a central element of the Putin regime's narrative has been the story of how the chaos of the 1990s under President Yeltsin was brought to an end once Putin came to power. The somewhat distorted official line has President Putin cracking down on the oligarchs' corruption and tax evasion in order to restore the proper functions of the state, ensuring that vast resources were no longer squirrelled away abroad and squandered but that a functioning fiscal system should be created, and the broad mass of the Russian people begin to benefit again from the wealth of the nation.

This is a neat story, not least because there is some substance to it. The early years of this century did indeed see the restoration of a functioning fiscal system in Russia and increasing amounts of money being collected by the state and spent on schools, hospitals, roads and so on. Both tax take and GDP increased and, during Putin's first two terms in office (2000–2008), spending on education went up from US$7.64 billion to US$68.1 billion and on healthcare from US$14.9 billion to US$103.3 billion. As the state coffers swelled during the energy boom of the 2000s, the Russian government rolled out its National Projects – each one focusing on a key area to be invested in and developed in order to modernise and enhance the services available to the Russian people. Although carried out within the framework of a market economy, such an approach was in some respects redolent of the old Soviet preference for plans and projects. Targets were set, resources were allocated, and a key figure in Moscow took responsibility – and some credit in official reporting – for the outcomes achieved. In 2005, National Projects for housing, healthcare, education and rural life were entrusted to the then First Deputy Prime Minister Dmitry Medvedev, providing him in the public mind with positive associations of state munificence ahead of his rise to the presidency in 2008.

The 'project approach' to such domestic priorities suits both the political culture and the political system of contemporary Russia. Russian political culture has a deeply ingrained sense of the state's role as overseer and provider that is inimical to Anglo-Saxon and neoliberal scepticism with regard to an overbearing state. This is not to say that Russians are not sceptical of their state or of those in power. After all, the history of Russia is replete with incidents – along the scale from ubiquitous dissatisfaction and grumbling to revolts and revolutions – stemming from dissatisfaction among the people with state corruption and rapacity. Nor can Russia's political culture in this regard be said to stem from decades of state-planning and totalitarian rule during the Soviet era; it pre-dates that, as even a passing knowledge of Imperial Russian history or a cursory reading of the works of Nikolai Gogol confirms. In 1836, Gogol wrote his comedy *The Government Inspector* on the theme of a corrupt and venal state power stealing from the people, and the Russian tradition of the political anecdote has consistently mined this particular comic seam. Such has been the scale of corruption in Russia in recent years that things moved beyond satire some time ago. In September 2016, a senior state official, Dmitry Zakharchenko, was arrested after police found 15 million rubles in cash (US$234,000) in his car. Further investigation at Zakharchenko's flat revealed stashes of €2 million and US$120 million, again in cash. According to reports in the Russian press, his salary over the previous few years amounted to no more than US$50,000. And Zakharchenko's job? Acting head of Russia's anti-corruption agency.

PUTIN: THE MAN AND THE PLAN

The presence of a central plan or project to improve important aspects of people's lives sits well within such a cultural setting. It sits well, too, with Russia's political system today. Although this chapter seeks to emphasise that President Putin does not – or, indeed, cannot – hold direct responsibility for everything that happens in Russia, it is nonetheless important to the way in which Russia's current system of government holds together that the President be seen to engage with and respond to the everyday needs of his people. One example of this is the annual presidential phone-in where, for several hours on live television, President Putin fields questions and requests from a range of selected citizens spread around the country. The lucky ones chosen from well over a million questions submitted are as likely to ask about some local, or even domestic, issue, as they are about grand political and international strategy. In one such *Direct Line with Putin* a young girl, perhaps confusing the President with Father Christmas, asked for a pretty dress, and not only was she rewarded with a lacy fairy-tale garment, but her family were flown to Moscow for tea with the President. In 2016, two female workers in a fish processing plant were chosen to appear on a direct video link with the President to complain that their wages had not been paid and that the local prosecutors were ignoring their grievances. The President intervened, telling Russia's Prosecutor General live on air to consider sacking his local staff if they did not pull their fingers out and resolve the women's problem.

This annual phone-in represents but one example of what is known as the 'manual control' system of governance, whereby President Putin is portrayed as the final arbiter and personalised Court of Appeal for the Russian people. It is a role suited to Russia's political culture, with Tsars and Soviet leaders alike sitting apparently above the fray, at the same time both all-powerful and yet unaware of – and therefore not to be blamed for – the malfeasances within the state structure over which they preside. In the starkest and darkest form of this element within Russia's political culture, victims of the Stalinist terror in the 1930s would protest to Stalin himself about their wrongful arrest and brutal ill-treatment, in the deluded belief that if only he knew what was going on he would mercifully intervene. As with most echoes of Soviet life apparent in contemporary Russia, Putin's veneration and interventions operate on a much lower level of magnitude.

The economic boom years of high energy prices boosting Russia's state budget in the first decade of this century are gone for now, and the National Projects faded into the background a little after the Medvedev presidency came to an end in 2012. They were not, however, mothballed, and nor was their project-oriented approach shelved. In 2016, President Putin established the Council on Strategic Development and Priority Projects to push forward on areas such as health, housing, education, roads, the environment, utilities and improvement of urban environment, productivity and support for small and medium enterprises and single-industry towns. In his inaugural speech to the Council, the President – mindful of falling energy prices and economic sanctions imposed on Russia after the annexation of Crimea in 2014 – emphasised that Russia's budget is seriously restricted compared to previous years, and that the designation of these key project areas under Council support ought not to be taken as permission to call on more state funding. His emphasis was on efficiency.

Despite this shift towards more straitened circumstances, however, the commitment to a project-based approach to improving performance in many of these vital areas remains. Russia's political culture and system are suited to the continuing notion that plans and projects 'from above' remain the best way to govern. Establishing the Council on Strategic Development and Priority Projects fits the standard pattern well; the government is seen to be doing something, the President publicly sets out his expectations for the work of the Council, responsibility for achieving the Council's aims is pushed down the chain of command to the Prime Minister and beyond to departmental ministers, and sporadic presidential intervention can be expected to dish out both blame and credit as the work of the Council proceeds.

It is somewhat ironic, then, that when – as this chapter intends – we make the effort to look at Russian politics in such a way as to emphasise aspects other than the role of President Vladimir Putin, we come back to emphasising the role of President Vladimir Putin. In many countries, however, the head of state or head of government will seek to set out broad policy positions in public, to associate themselves with success and to distance themselves from failure. Russia is not unique in this regard. It is in Russia's government, though, that the hard policy yards are covered. The distinctive roles of President and government in Russia are set out in the constitution, which dates from 1993. Whereas the President, as head of state, takes responsibility for international affairs and is commander-in-chief of the armed forces, it is the government that, according to the constitution, develops and implements policy with regard to the state budget, education, health, the environment, social security and culture. The President is in charge – after all, he appoints the Prime Minister – but it is in the ministerial team and their departments that policy development and expertise lies. The 'manual control' of one man is OK for headlines, but in these everyday policy areas, consistent and coherent nationwide policies are more important even if less widely reported.

THE SIZE OF THE RUSSIAN STATE

This chapter began by considering the Pikalyovo incident as indicative of various aspects of Russian political life. The specific example of the single-industry towns illustrates the broader point that – for entirely understandable reasons – most external observers of Russia note the headlines when crises arise and Putin intervenes, but have less of a sense of the day-to-day functioning of Russia's governmental machine. Russia's civil service grew dramatically – some estimates say fourfold – during this century's opening decade, as the wealth and functions of the state developed. The early 1990s had seen a flight from state employment with the weak state no longer able to pay wages, and millions of former apparatchiks entered what one might loosely call the 'private sector' in order to find a living. The trend reversed in the twenty-first century when the ranks of the public sector swelled once more with employees attracted by such diverse enticements as job stability, a decent wage, work more suited to the well-educated, and – in some sectors – the opportunities for enrichment via the corrupt use of position. According to the OECD, by 2010 more than 20 per cent of the Russian workforce had jobs in 'the general government sector' (a wide definition including all institutions at federal, regional and municipal level with political and economic regulatory functions or engaged in the production of public goods). The Russian newspaper *Komsomolskaya pravda* sceptically analysed official government data from 2013. Its report noted that adding regional and municipal civil servants to the figure of 38,000 federal government employees produced a total of 1.1 million, and that this could be doubled if one included all the support staff (cleaners, caterers, drivers and so on). It further argued that the number of people whose salaries depended directly on the state budget rose to a remarkable 33.6 million out of a working age population of around 85 million, if we include the armed forces, the police, other security forces, those who work in the health and education sectors and workers in enterprises wholly or partially owned by the state. That's a remarkably large state sector for a country that made the decision to drop socialism in favour of market capitalism a quarter of a century ago.

Aside from the familiar economic questions around how to pay for so large a budget-dependent workforce many of whom are not themselves creating wealth, two interesting insights into Russian politics today emerge from this consideration of the number of state employees. The first has to do with the interdependent nature of Russian politics at the macro level. A fairly standard view within the democratic transition literature paints the emergence of a middle class as an important element in the consolidation of democracy, as they develop networks and norms conducive to democratic values. Such was the standard assessment several decades ago, although more recent research muddies so straightforward a view by considering complicating factors such as income inequality, gradations within the middle class, tensions between a preference for democracy and a preference for stability. In the Russian case, the fact that so large a proportion of what we might term the middle class depends on the state for its income may undermine the notion held dear by many observers during the anti-Putin demonstrations of 2011–2012 and the anti-corruption demonstrations of 2017 that Russia's growing middle class inevitably represents a source of anti-regime feeling. The size of the state creates dependence networks also at the municipal and regional levels. When the federal state could not resource the regions in the 1990s, the centrifugal forces of separatism were strong. Today resource flows and federal funding, linked together by the political institutions of the 'power vertical' (see Chapter Five), fortify state unity.

THE STRUCTURE OF RUSSIA'S GOVERNMENT

The second, and slightly contrary, attribute of Russian politics that comes to mind when considering the size of the Russian state has to do with the division of labour and authority inside Russian politics, and returns us to the theme of the centrality or otherwise of Vladimir Putin. On the one hand, what has always been obvious is that so large a country as Russia requires a large cohort of skilled and well-educated civil servants organised into the appropriate institutional frameworks at federal and regional levels. In other words, policies are developed and implemented across the range of policy areas to be found in any developed country without the 'manual control' of President Putin. He exercises his presidential authority through an oversight function that includes formal meetings with his Prime Minister, each sitting either side of the heavy wooden desk in the President's Kremlin office, with press and TV cameras present so that the process can be seen to be carried out. The content of such meetings may involve the President demonstrating his authority over the government by criticising, for example, governmental failure to solve this or that problem, or to follow some presidential instruction. During the Dmitry Medvedev interregnum of 2008–2012, when Putin was Medvedev's Prime Minister, the formal roles and indeed seating positions changed about, with President Medvedev even on occasion seen to be criticising the performance of Russia's government, and by implication its head, Prime Minister Putin. With twenty-one government ministries, overseen not only by their ministers and the Prime Minister but also by an intermediate level of – at the time of writing, though this may vary in its detail – one First Deputy Prime Minister (Igor Shuvalov) and eight Deputy Prime Ministers, the process of government tends towards a technocratic competence-based approach across most areas of activity for most of the time.

The sorts of issues that take up most of the government's attention in Russia do not tend to hit the international headlines. In comparison with spying, military threat, hacking, doping, poisoning, great power competition and all the other issues that spring to the fore when the international media deal with matters Russian, the day-to-day affairs of government might seem rather dull. They make up, however, the substance of everyday life. For the Russian people, living standards and welfare, schools and hospitals, roads and water pipes, all of these come higher up the list of priorities than do cheating hammer throwers and the US presidential elections. Taking a look at its formal annual report illustrates well the primary concerns of the Russian government. In mid-April 2017, Russia's Prime Minister Dmitry Medvedev, in accordance with constitutional requirements, presented that year's annual report on government performance to the lower house of parliament: the State Duma. A month before that, President Putin had held an extended meeting with government ministers that covered the same questions as that formal report. Addressing parliament, Medvedev noted that in the preceding year the Duma had adopted almost 300 legislative bills proposed by the government, and highlighted among them laws on the quality of forensics, road safety and reducing traffic congestion. He then proceeded at some length to outline the achievements of his government in areas such as the economy, business, demographics, health care, education, labour, social security, industry, sport, agriculture, the energy sector, construction and housebuilding. Highlights included the highest level of life expectancy in Russia's history (seventy-two years) and – related – Russia's success in climbing into the World Health Organization's top ten when it comes to progress in fighting heart and lung diseases and diabetes. Long-term projects saw progress, such as the development of rural schools and medical provision, and the establishment of a mortgage market in Russia. The Prime Minister did not ignore the more headline-worthy developments, such as a 10 per cent increase in defence sector production or the challenges of incorporating Crimea into the Russian Federation, but these were covered almost in passing within the wider report.

RUSSIA'S SECURITY COUNCIL

There is a certain reassuring dullness about the foregoing description of technocratic governance in Russia. It is not for the most part the stuff of headlines, of great power politics, of dictatorial control. Nor, however, is it the full picture. When it comes to those matters of state that are either constitutionally under the direct control of the President – war and peace, security, international relations – or that the President and his inner circle want to elevate into their area of competence, then formal procedures come up against, or merge with, a less formalised approach that centres around President Putin, his friends and his advisers. Some have adopted the term 'the collective Putin' to capture a sense of this group of friends and colleagues who are the key decision-makers inside Russian politics. Their influence straddles the border between formal structures and informal authority. Leading British scholar of Russian politics Richard Sakwa speaks of

Russia's 'dual state' to illustrate that it is not simply a matter of the formal structures comprising a Potemkin village of institutional normality behind which we find a mess of President Putin's oligarchic and security service cronies exercising power haphazardly. It is rather that the formal institutions and the informal networks *both* carry policy-making force.

The single most significant collective decision-making body inside Russian politics is the Security Council of the Russian Federation. There is no doubting the formal status of the Security Council, since it was established on a permanent basis by Russia's 1993 constitution. But its constitutional standing has left plenty of leeway for the head of state to shape it according to his preferences, and for the Security Council itself to spread its authority and area of competence in line with these preferences. The constitution merely establishes the council's existence. Russia's Presidents have decided its influence – since it is an advisory body – its membership and its trappings.

If we were to search for contemporary Russia's equivalent of the British cabinet, or of the Soviet Union's politburo, then in functional – as opposed to institutional – terms, this is as near as we get. The offices of the Security Council and its substantial staff are situated on Old Square, a stone's throw from the Kremlin, where its meetings take place. Symbolically, these offices used to belong to the Central Committee of the Communist Party of the Soviet Union. Russia's Security Council is chaired by the President and meets regularly to discuss the key matters of state. The remit of security represents a useful catch-all, since almost anything can be represented as a security threat and the tendency to do precisely this has run wild in the high politics of Russia for most of this century. Economic security, information security, even spiritual security; all these and more have become commonplace in Russian political discourse.

When meeting in full session, as it does a few times a year, the Security Council of the Russian Federation has around twenty-five members. In the abandonment of any pretence at a formal separation of powers between the executive, legislature and judiciary, it draws together government ministers, the presidential plenipotentiaries to Russia's Federal Districts, military and security service leaders, the municipal bosses of Moscow and St Petersburg, the Federal Prosecutor, and the speakers of both parliamentary chambers. More often, however, the President holds shorter and less formal meetings, not always reported in the media, with about a dozen 'permanent members' of his Security Council. It is here that President Putin sits with the head of his presidential administration, the heads of the ministries of defence, internal affairs, foreign affairs, the Prime Minister, the parliamentary speakers and Russia's security service chiefs to make policy on the most significant issues affecting Russia's security. In recent years these men – and one woman, Valentina Matvienko, the speaker of the upper house of parliament – have discussed the headline questions facing Russia. Crimea, Ukraine, Syria, relations with NATO, doping in sport, security in the Baltic region, the Russian economy and so on have all been the subject of 'deep discussion', in the words of presidential spokesman Dmitry Peskov.

PUTIN'S INNER CIRCLE

In 2007, a political thriller was published in Moscow with the none-too-subtle title of *Polonium for Breakfast*. Drawing on the murder in London in 2006 of Alexander Litvinenko – a former Russian security services agent working for the British security services – the opening paragraphs of the book imagine a scene in the President's office in the Kremlin shortly after a Russian dissident has been found poisoned by polonium in London. The plot revolves around the question of who was behind the murder. *Polonium for Breakfast* begins like this. 'The President lifted the receiver of the internal phone and barked: Send Patrushev to me.' (*Zavtrak s poloniem*, Natalya Aleksandrova.)

The Patrushev in question is Secretary of the Russian Security Council Nikolai Patrushev who, at that time, was the director of the FSB, Russia's internal security service, a position he had inherited from Vladimir Putin in 1999. The opening lines of this Russian-language thriller by the prolific Natalya Aleksandrova were echoed in far more sober and serious form almost a decade later, in the final chapter of 'The Litvinenko Inquiry: Report into the death of Alexander Litvinenko' (2016) written by Sir Robert Owen, ordered by the House of Commons and published on behalf of Her Majesty's Stationery Office. Adopting an unusually suspenseful style for so sombre and formal a document, Sir Robert began the final chapter thus:

My finding that Mr Litvinenko was killed at the direction of the FSB gives rise to one further issue. At what level of seniority was the plan to kill Mr Litvinenko authorised? Was Mr Patrushev, the then head of the FSB, aware of the operation? Was President Putin aware of the operation?

In true thriller style, rather than the careful evidence-focused prose of a legal report, the author leaves the big reveal to the chapter's final sentence. He also – though he needs to employ a somewhat unusual passive phrasing to do so – leaves the name of the man he believes to be ultimately responsible to the chapter's final word. And, even then, he injects a little adverbial doubt. Sir Robert concludes that 'the FSB operation to kill Mr Litvinenko was probably approved by Mr Patrushev and also by President Putin'.

Patrushev has been Secretary of the Security Council of the Russian Federation since 2008. Like Putin, Patrushev was born in Leningrad in the early 1950s and, like Putin, he joined the KGB in that same city in the mid-1970s. When Vladimir Putin became acting President in 1999, concern that he was not sufficiently well known either domestically or internationally led to the swift publication of a book – *First Person* – consisting of conversations with him and those who knew him well. Pressed to name people with whom he'd formed a particular bond in his working life, the then somewhat bashful new Russian leader revealed that there were three people whom he considered close and supportive colleagues. Patrushev made this short list. The other two were Dmitry Medvedev and Sergei Ivanov.

It is in figures like Patrushev, Medvedev and Ivanov that the boundary between formal and informal blurs. They have each one held formal positions at the highest level of the Russian state. Nikolai Patrushev, as we have seen, became head of the FSB then Secretary of the Security Council of the Russian Federation. Sergei Ivanov has also been Secretary of the Security Council, before becoming Minister of Defence and later – until 2016 – Head of the Presidential Administration. Medvedev of course made it to the very top, the presidency of the Russian Federation. Talented though they are in their particular ways, these men rose to power with Putin and this close friendship has been instrumental in their elevation.

Perhaps the single most pivotal event of the Putin presidency was the annexation of Crimea in 2014 (explored in much more detail in Chapter Eight). In a TV interview the following year, Vladimir Putin gave his version of events. He told of a sleepless night at his residence outside Moscow when, in the company of his four closest advisers, he began to formulate the idea of bringing Crimea into the Russian Federation. Two out of those four were Sergei Ivanov and Nikolai Patrushev. The other two were Defence Minister Sergei Shoigu and Head of the FSB Alexander Bortnikov who, like Putin and Patrushev, had joined the KGB in Leningrad in the mid-1970s. Such a style of government is by no means unique in itself, as anyone who has read accounts of Tony Blair's 'sofa' government and the decision-making process that led the United Kingdom into the Iraq war of 2003 would recognise. Comparisons of process should not, however, lead to conclusions of duplication. In the established democracy of the UK, official enquiries probed the process, the British Prime Minister was subject to the will of his party and colleagues in leaving office, and his party was subject to the will of the British people in parliament when it lost power in 2010. Russia is not an established democracy. For all its democratic institutions, Russia's polity lacks such working processes of democratic accountability.

In 2015 the young Russian TV journalist and presenter Mikhail Zygar, who had made his name on the somewhat anti-establishment channel *Dozhd* (Rain), published a book that was soon to become a bestseller in Russia. Published in English as *All the Kremlin's Men: Inside the Court of Vladimir Putin* and translated into Polish, German, Bulgarian, Finnish and Chinese, Zygar's book provides – in the words of its Russian edition's subtitle – a short history of contemporary Russia. Its structural device is to tell this history in a series of chapters, each one organised around a prominent figure in the Putin regime. Its central message is commendably nuanced. Inside Russia's ruling regime, Putin is pivotal but neither, even in the limited temporal sense, omnipotent nor omniscient. In other words, it is around him that the regime's power revolves, and through him that power and its accompanying wealth are distributed. But the simplistic view that every decision made in Russia is part of some carefully planned operation run by a cohesive regime does not stack up. The complex of institutional framework, personal caprice and the insistent background hum of the mood of the Russian masses shapes what happens inside Russian politics.

There remains one name not yet mentioned in this chapter, and yet it is both important in and illustrative of the working of the Putin regime. Igor Sechin is yet another Leningrader to rise to power with Putin. His personal brand is loyalty to the President and ruthlessness in operating within the twilight zone of state-private-personal business activity. Sechin worked for Putin in St Petersburg in the 1990s and came with him to Moscow. He has been described at different times by different analysts as Putin's number two and the second most important man in Russia, despite his highest formal political position being Deputy Prime Minister between 2008 and 2012 under Prime Minister Vladimir Putin and during the presidency of Dmitry Medvedev.

The informal side of Russian politics means that, often, the person matters more than the position. The overlap between formal state position, personal influence and the world of business has been embodied in Sechin. His hard-line political and business style apparently put him at odds with Medvedev over many years. Sechin was seen as the chief of the *siloviki* (security forces) in the regime. He has a background in the Soviet military and is older than the entirely civilian and outwardly more cerebral Medvedev, who professes a more liberal perspective. During the 'tandem' of power in Russia between 2008 and 2012, in formal terms Medvedev dominated the power structure as President and Head of

State. In practice, he owed his position to Putin, at best shared power with him, and in the eyes of many remained Putin's de facto subordinate. That being the case, Sechin as one of several Deputy Prime Ministers was all the more subordinate to Medvedev in formal terms. But as Putin's right-hand man he maintained significant informal power and perhaps – if these things could indeed be measured – greater influence than his President in some areas of activity.

In terms of business activity, the intersection of political power and the riches of the business world stand stark in Russian practice. Between 2000 and 2008, Medvedev served as chairman of the board of the massive gas company Gazprom. From 2004 onwards, Sechin was chair of the board of the Rosneft oil company, and later became its president in 2012. Medvedev gained a reputation as being somewhat hands-off when it came to the business of Gazprom, although he engaged more in the political side such as negotiations on pricing with Ukraine. Sechin, on the other hand, is seen as very much instrumental in terms of developing Rosneft, the company that gained the assets of the Yukos Oil Company owned by oligarch and oppositionist Mikhail Khodorkovsky, who was imprisoned between 2003 and 2013.

The enigma of Russia's ruling regime requires multiple perspectives to begin to grasp it. A description of its institutions serves some purpose. They are democratic in design and, although their democratic frame has fundamental deficiencies in functionally democratic content, Russia's institutions do provide formal shape and technocratic substance. These institutions and their positions, however, do not so much bestow power as they are occupied by it. The political power of the Putin regime moves in and around the institutional frame. Although certainly not alone in this respect when it comes to the leaders of nations, those who rule contemporary Russia too often appear to act as if these positions are their own property, rather than seeing themselves as public servants temporarily holding power at the behest of the Russian people.

CHAPTER FOUR

RUSSIAN POLITICS BEYOND THE REGIME

LOOKING FOR LEADERS

It is a tactic of authoritarian leaders to appear so indispensable that the thought of their not being in charge seems inconceivable. The longer a leader retains power, the more the system shapes itself around the personality and policies of its head. 'Leaderism' has particular resonance in Russian politics. During the Soviet era, it was a pejorative term ideologically speaking; after all, the etymological differentiation between communism and leaderism could not be starker – a communal, collective 'state of all the people' as the later Soviet Union declared itself to be, versus – and in reaction to – the capture of that state by a single predominant leader, Joseph Stalin, between 1928 and 1953. The Putin regime is no Stalinist totalitarian dictatorship, but it is 'leaderist' in nature, since the regime has captured the state and appears to treat it as a personal possession. Given a head start by Russia's super-presidential constitution (1993) – which is about as presidential as it is possible to be while still remaining within the democratic pale – Putin stuck to the letter of the constitution by stepping down in 2008, having completed the two consecutive terms allowed. For the next four years he served as Prime Minister to placeman-protégé President Dmitry Medvedev in what became known as a 'tandemocracy', because, although Medvedev formally had the extensive powers of the presidency, Putin's role as Prime Minister, his support in the parliament, his public standing and his personal influence over Medvedev and the Russian élite left him in the eyes of many as the ultimate decision-maker in Russia.

As it happened, although the tone of President Medvedev was more liberal than that of Putin, no great policy differences arose. Medvedev used his period in office to introduce the first major reform to the Russian Constitution: namely, lengthening of the presidential term to six years instead of four. In September 2011, despite being previously coy on the matter, Medvedev and Putin announced that Putin planned to return to the presidency in 2012. The idea that the position of head of state in a supposedly democratic country could be swapped in élite deals of this type emphasised how far Russia had backslidden from its self-proclaimed transition to an open democracy. When Putin resumed the presidency, he had the potential of another two terms to rule over Russia. Having come to power in 2000 and served two four-year terms until 2008 before becoming Prime Minister from

2008 to 2012, he could remain as President for a further two six-year terms until 2024.

Given that Russia has rejected an open democracy in favour of a 'leaderist' political regime, it makes sense that when we try to look beyond Putin, the question arises: who else could fill this role? Within the regime, it is possible to find experienced figures or – as explained in Chapter Five – younger rising representatives of a new generation who can be groomed for power and have their image burnished by the media. After all, that is how Medvedev became President. It is much more difficult, however, even if we can imagine the fall of the current regime, to find such a figure among opposition forces.

The leaders of the two main and relatively supine parliamentary opposition parties, the Communists and the Liberal Democratic Party of Russia – Gennady Zyuganov and Vladimir Zhirinovsky respectively – have held those roles since the early 1990s and seem comfortable enough with the occasional carping at the regime combined with no serious efforts towards, or expectation of, ever replacing it. Beyond the 'virtual opposition' of these parliamentary parties, the anti-Putin liberals who enjoy a profile in the West – for example, the 'three Ks', former world chess champion Garry Kasparov, exiled ex-oligarch Mikhail Khodorkovsky and Putin's first Prime Minister (2000–2004) Mikhail Kasyanov – are unlikely ever to win mass support in Russia. It is too easy for their opponents to tar them with a combination of corruption and unpatriotic pro-Western conspiracy.

ALEXEI NAVALNY

But there is one staunch opponent of the Putin regime who looks more promising in terms of presidential attributes. Alexei Navalny is a tall, good-looking and confident figure. He is not associated with the baleful 1990s, having emerged on the scene as a Moscow-based blogger at the end of this century's first decade. Born in 1976, Navalny came of age after the Soviet Union had collapsed and has the sort of appeal that can attract young post-Soviet supporters. His initial fame came as an anti-corruption campaigner, and – as Chapter Six makes clear – if there is any topic on which the Putin regime is vulnerable to otherwise supportive Russian citizens, it is corruption. As for the idea that Navalny is a Western stooge betraying his country, a line Putin supporters happily spin, among Russian liberals – broadly supportive of Navalny – the one concern that they have about him is that he occasionally seems a little too nationalist for their tastes. The nationalist feeling of the Russian population, particularly in a post-Crimea world, is such that in any democratic election a reputation as a Russian patriot represents a *sine qua non* of success.

In December 2016, a few months after turning forty, Alexei Navalny became the first Russian political figure to declare his intention to run for the presidency in 2018. His announcement contained the same message that has recurred throughout his brief political career: namely, let us rid ourselves of the corrupt Putin regime that has stolen power and riches and uses the Russian state as its own personal possession. In his early public profile as an anti-corruption campaigner, Navalny bought shares in a number of major energy companies with close ties to the state, so that he could ask questions as a 'share-holder activist'. He thus made himself unpopular with many members of the élite and succeeded in revealing a series of embarrassing facts about the property and wealth of state officials whose salaries would come nowhere near the level required for these holdings. After highlighting the connection between ill-gotten gains and political power, Navalny moved more overtly into politics. In 2011, Navalny coined the phrase 'the party of crooks and thieves' to describe Putin's party United Russia. It resonated with so many people that it became a meme during the parliamentary election campaign of 2011 and the presidential election of 2012. Supporters of United Russia unwittingly helped to spread the phrase by protesting loudly at its first usage by Navalny, thereby inadvertently drawing attention to its pithy precision. Opponents of the regime used it on car stickers, or displayed on placards at protest rallies. 'The party of crooks and thieves' morphed into an acronym (PZhV, in Russian ПЖВ) that is still used and understood in Russia's political discourse today. Its effectiveness lies both in the succinctness of the phrase itself, and also in the fact that it is not a direct attack on Putin himself – who still retains great popularity and respect in Russia – but attacks the more amorphous and widely acceptable target of the corrupt political élite. After all, who could not be against corruption? Particularly in Russia, with its strongly egalitarian and communal sensitivities and a ruling regime whose founding narrative emphasised the renewal of Russia after the venal and immoral oligarch-led chaos of the 1990s.

In spring 2017, Alexei Navalny's campaign moved up a gear. His Anti-Corruption Foundation released a video making allegations of corruption against the Prime Minister – and former President of Russia – Dmitry Medvedev. The video had a theme familiar to anyone who has followed such accusations of venality and sleaze in Russia's post-Soviet years. The tale presented was one of former classmates acting as front men, oligarchs paying for influence, officials turning a blind eye, Potemkin organisations with proxy ownership and so on. So far, so regrettably normal. The Medvedev video, however, surpassed what had gone before in several significant ways. To start with, its target was a recent head of state who now occupied the second most powerful position in the country. Short of going for Vladimir Putin, it doesn't get any higher than this. As Navalny knew, attacking Putin would have been counter-productive, because of the popularity and status of the President among the Russian people and the response of the regime to such an attack would likely have been of a ferocity beyond what was borne after the Medvedev investigation.

Significant, too, was that although the nature of the accusations against Prime Minister Medvedev was of a familiar type, the detailed allegations themselves were new, specific and wide-ranging. Claims were made about vast properties and estates in Russia and abroad that had allegedly been bought and maintained on behalf of the head of the government. These claims were accompanied by detailed denunciations of the methods employed in the building up of what the Anti-Corruption Foundation termed 'the corrupt empire of the chairman of the government of the Russian Federation and the United Russia party'. Finally, this video denunciation stood out for the slickness of its presentation. Almost fifty minutes in length, it was presented by Navalny himself with all the skill of a practised media performer. Jacket off, the sleeves of his pale blue shirt neatly rolled to just below his elbows and navy-blue tie in place, the tall and confident figure of Alexei Navalny addresses the viewer from his seat in front of a bookshelf-covered wall in a room that has the look of trendy, urban loft-cum-office. It's a relaxed setting and, despite the seriousness of the subject, there's a lightness and humour in the presentation. The video is broken up into sections as he deals with separate aspects of the allegations. The opportunities of the visual medium are exploited to the full; it includes not just photos of documents and properties, but drone footage of vast estates and houses, interviews with locals and graphics purporting to represent the web of connections behind it all. It's choreographed to a T, as Navalny seems to pluck words and pictures out of the air and send them scrolling as graphics across the screen.

At the end of the video, Navalny turns his attention away from Medvedev and to the twofold response that he wants to see. First, he encourages his viewers to disseminate the video. Declaring that 'yes, television is fully controlled by this mafia… but we can overcome censorship by passing information from person to person', he urges everyone to send a link of the video to their friends, to tell their relatives and to fight any way they can. Second, and perhaps more significantly, the video ends by drawing attention to Navalny's candidacy in the 2018 presidential election.

It is, of course, difficult to make informed judgements on the accuracy of the allegations contained in the Anti-Corruption Foundation's investigation into Dmitry Medvedev. What is not in doubt, though, is the striking impact that this investigation had in Russia in the weeks following its release. In particular, in late March 2017, a day of protest saw demonstrations in more than eighty towns and cities across Russia, from St Petersburg to Vladivostok. Participation in a score or more of these numbered in the thousands, and estimates in Moscow put the number of demonstrators at around 20,000. In response, the authorities arrested hundreds, including Navalny. In the days following, supportive media and social media published photos of uniformed, helmeted police moving against demonstrators. The emphasis of coverage in the aftermath of these demonstrations was on the youthfulness of many participants, with supporters of the protests talking of a new generation coming of age and finally rising up against a stagnant and corrupt regime.

The demonstrations of March 2017 and the broader anti-corruption campaign of Alexei Navalny differ in generational terms from previous protest movements. The fear of the Putin regime as the first decade of this century progressed was that there might be a Russian version of the 'Colour Revolutions' that had overthrown governments in Georgia, Ukraine and Kyrgyzstan between 2003 and 2005. The banner under which such protests took place was democracy and freedom. In a sense, these calls for democracy and freedom can be seen as the after-shock of the Soviet collapse. Indeed, in 1991, people across the former Soviet Union were told that democracy was theirs, and when it did not always turn out that way, fierce protest occasionally arose in an attempt to regain the promise.

A Colour Revolution was never likely to happen in Russia. One reason for this is the genuine popularity of the Putin regime among the majority of Russians. Another is that the brutal experience of socio-economic collapse in the 1990s became associated in the minds of many with democracy. A third barrier to the spread of pro-democracy activism in Russia has been the notion, increasingly promoted by the authorities, that liberal democracy is a Western concept – or, more aggressively, a Western plot – that ought not to be imposed on Russia. Calls to rise up in support of democracy had small chance of rallying the patriotic masses. Nonetheless, that did not stop the Putin regime from organising to prevent such uprisings. The nearest Russia came to such a pro-democracy uprising was in between the parliamentary elections of December 2011 and the inauguration of Vladimir Putin for his third presidential term in May 2012. Angered by what they believed to be electoral fraud and frustrated at the return of Putin to power, thousands of people took part in demonstrations in over ninety towns and cities across Russia. There was also a series of mass demonstrations in Moscow – some with the permission of the authorities, some without – culminating in the now infamous Bolotnaya Square demonstration on 6 May 2012, the eve of the presidential inauguration. With a rally numbering around 20,000, violence between the police and the protesters flared up, and demonstrators accused the police of overt provocation. Bloody street battles ensued, and tens of demonstrators were subsequently charged with and convicted of rioting. A number of prominent opposition leaders had their houses searched, and the Bolotnaya case became seen in Russia and abroad as marking a new level of official crackdown against opponents of the regime.

In March 2017, the protests differed in several ways from those of five years earlier. Whatever their long-term aims, the protest organisers played a blinder in alighting on corruption as the object of their ire. This is no political theme per se, but, as was seen in the United Kingdom during the parliamentary expenses scandal of 2009, corruption stirs the emotions of people across the country. It's a lot more difficult for the Putin regime to effectively smear anti-corruption demonstrators as being tools of the West intent on introducing alien concepts into Russia; not least because the regime itself has repeatedly spoken out against corruption and launched campaigns ostensibly aimed at cleaning up the system. In speaking out against corruption and being careful not – at the time of writing, at least – to overtly target

President Putin himself, the anti-sleaze campaigners inoculate themselves against accusations that they are somehow anti-patriotic or anti-Russia. Such accusations are thrown at them, but their rationale lacks robustness. The relative youth of Navalny and many of the protesters likewise represents a shift beyond the previous 'democrats versus statists', 'pro-Westerners versus patriots' dividing lines. The political life of this rising generation has little but hand-me-down knowledge of the chaotic and economically difficult 1990s, let alone of the Soviet era. That was the era of their parents; this is the era of the rising generation who have known nothing but Putin as their President.

Perceiving Navalny to be on to a winner with his focus on corruption, the authorities have sought to beat him with his own stick. In 2012 Russia's Investigative Committee – led by Alexander Bastrykin, a university classmate of President Putin in the Law Department of the Leningrad State University back in the 1970s – charged Navalny with embezzlement relating to a timber company in Kirov, almost a thousand kilometres east of Moscow. After a lengthy court case, Navalny was initially sentenced to five years in prison – a sentencing that occurred the day after he was registered as a candidate for the Moscow mayoral election. With surprising rapidity, however, and after Navalny had called for a boycott of that election by Muscovites, the sentence was suspended. The prosecutor's office declared that to imprison Navalny would prevent him from exercising his rights of equal access to the electorate. Navalny eventually received 27 per cent of the vote, coming second to the regime candidate – and now Mayor of Moscow – Sergei Sobyanin. That suspended sentence still hangs over him as a potential means of excluding his candidacy from the 2018 presidential election as well, of course, as a threat to his liberty.

Alexei Navalny began campaigning for the 2018 presidential election earlier than any other potential candidate, with the dual aim of increasing name recognition and creating a situation where action taken against him by the authorities might be construed as interference in the democratic process. For all the attention that he receives in the international media and for all the enthusiasm and anger with which his exposé of Prime Minister Medvedev's alleged corruption was received by a segment of Russia's youth, a reliable opinion poll in April 2017 demonstrated how far he is from actual power, even were Russia to operate a free and fair electoral system. When pollsters asked for whom would you vote were there to be a presidential election this Sunday, Vladimir Putin was way at the front with an 83 per cent rating. In joint fourth place came Alexei Navalny, with a rating of just 2 per cent.

THE IN-SYSTEM OPPOSITION

In the above-mentioned opinion poll from April 2017, sitting between Putin and Navalny on the list of preferred presidential candidates was Vladimir Zhirinovsky (5 per cent) and Gennady Zyuganov (4 per cent). As noted above, these two figures are the dinosaurs of Russian politics, survivors from the first post-Soviet elections of the early 1990s. In theory, Zhirinovsky and his Liberal Democratic Party of Russia are situated on the nationalist far-right, while Zyuganov and his Communist Party of the Russian Federation are on the far left. In fact, both of these parties function as support for the existing system, opposing more in rhetoric than in reality and seemingly complicit in an acceptance that the ruling regime retains its position.

Distinction should be made between the parliamentary and presidential elections in which these parties participate. In the former, with 450 seats up for grabs, of which 225 are distributed by a system of proportional representation, voting for the parties of the in-system opposition does allow voters to express some dissatisfaction with the ruling regime – albeit that, as explained in Chapter Two, parliamentary elections in Russia cannot change the ruling regime. In the 2016 parliamentary election, both the Liberal Democrats and the Communists received 13 per cent of the vote in the PR section of the ballot – although, once diluted by the constituency – that had diminished to around 9 per cent of the seats each.

Why then do they bother? What is in it for these two parties? Or even for the third in-system opposition party A Just Russia, set up with the backing of the Kremlin and polling 6 per cent in the 2016 election? They present themselves as opposition, but really they perform a useful function for the ruling regime. They demonstrate the existence of a multi-party system while remaining relatively supine. It certainly is easy to be cynical about the in-system opposition parties – and from the perspective of those whose focus is on removing the ruling regime and renewing democracy in Russia, they are more hindrance than ally. A revealing account of the meeting between President Putin and the leaders of the in-system opposition parties after the parliamentary election of December 2016 showed them haggling over minor positions and privileges, more in the role of supplicant than opponent. At the same time, though, their programmes do correspond to the political positions of nearly a third of Russia's voters, their participation in electoral campaigns allows policy alternatives to be expressed, they fill almost a quarter of parliamentary seats and 8 per cent of constituencies have a representative who is not a member of Putin's United Russia party.

If at least some case can be made for not dismissing the role of in-system opposition when it comes to parliamentary elections, the winner-takes-all nature of presidential elections represents a different matter. We are more than two decades from the closely fought Boris Yeltsin versus Gennady Zyuganov presidential contest of 1996: an election that required a second round and was justifiably billed as a system-defining moment. Since then, the candidacies of Vladimir Zhirinovsky and Gennady Zyuganov – both of whom took a break for the 2004 presidential election, but have contested all of the others – have seemed perfunctory and electorally pointless, serving the regime's purpose of multi-candidacy while offering increasingly tired tropes of tainted opposition to the electorate. Communist voters come disproportionately from the older generation; and, as they die off, so support for the party declines. Although Gennady Zyuganov received 17 per cent of the vote in the 2012 presidential election, by mid-2017 he was polling around 4 per cent. If ever there were symbols of a fossilised political system and political parties, the seemingly ageless 'twins' of Russia's in-system opposition – Vladimir Zhirinovsky and Gennady Zyuganov – are those symbols.

HOW RUSSIA'S RULING REGIME RESPONDS TO OPPOSITION

Russia's political system is one that seeks to show the attributes of electoral democracy without risking the power of the ruling regime. That being the case, rather than be seen to overtly interfere in electoral processes, the regime's preference is for control to be implemented through routine engagement with in-system political parties and inconspicuous manipulation of influential factors such as media output, electoral rules and polling day activities. In cases when such manipulation is insufficient, or simply when the authorities' habitual assumption of power shows its face too readily, more blunt instruments – such as police action, legal processes and targeted legislation – can confront political opponents.

Control of the media in contemporary Russia rarely takes the crass propagandistic form employed by old-style authoritarian regimes, such as the Soviet Communist Party. It is a little more subtle than that, focusing particularly on mass consumption TV channels and subjects of especial importance to the regime. Self-censorship plays a key role, as journalists develop an awareness of no-go areas. For example, coverage of Vladimir Putin's personal and business life is out, as is – in the mainstream at least – vehement criticism of events and policy decisions deemed vital to the national interest, such as the Chechen wars and the incorporation of Crimea into the Russian Federation. Journalists concerned for their careers are only too aware of numerous examples where reporters and editors have been sacked by their bosses shortly after overstepping some undefined but widely sensed line. Way back in 2004, the editor of the well-known newspaper *Izvestia* lost his job within days of his publication carrying hard-hitting photographs of and content about the terrorist seizure of a school in Beslan and the brutal deaths of children as the authorities brought the siege to an end (the Beslan tragedy is discussed in more detail in Chapter Five). More recently, in 2016 three senior editors from the respected business media group RBC were removed from their posts amidst reports that RBC's billionaire owner, Mikhail Prokhorov, had been leant on by Kremlin officials, concerned over investigative reporting probing the wealth of figures close to the President, and even – by being the major Russian outlet when it came to coverage of the Panama papers – of the President himself. These are but two examples of a fairly regularly reported pattern, whereby Russia's ruling regime does not seek to control everything in the media, but rather to indicate limits, influence content and step in as it deems necessary. Opposition politicians and critical journalism are by no means banned from the media per se. Indeed, the many hours of electoral debates on Russian television ahead of 2016's Duma election were at least as robust as similar coverage in the United States and Europe, with both in-system and non-systemic opposition politicians taking part. A sense exists, however, that the authorities can and will step in to control the media as they feel the need.

Manipulation of electoral rules represents another way in which the influence of opposition forces can be controlled largely 'under the radar'. At the headline level of election results and candidates, the Russian system boasts the sort of stability that the Putin regime prides itself on having brought to the country. But the process by which such stable outcomes are achieved is one in which Russia's elections themselves are in constant flux. Every election brings multiple rule changes, new procedures and new efficiency-driven refinements to make things run in a regime-friendly way. During the post-Soviet era, the parliamentary term has been, at various points, two years, four years and – since 2011 – five years. Parliamentary and presidential elections for most of this period took place within a few months of each other, but now that the presidential term has been changed from four years to six years the temporal relationship between the two will vary each time. The electoral system itself changes regularly too. Between 1993 and 2003 the Duma was elected under a half single-mandate, half proportional representation combination. After independent candidates won more than 100 constituency seats in 2003, the next two elections adopted an entirely proportional, party-list vote that facilitated centralised control. Then in 2016, the United Russia party having been firmly established in constituencies across the country, Russia's parliamentary electoral system reverted back to the previous 50/50 mix, again benefiting the ruling regime as United Russia won 60 per cent of its seats from single-mandate constituencies. On top of all that, detailed and regularly changing procedures for registering candidates and parties also provide opportunities for the authorities to prevent unwanted names from appearing on the ballot paper while citing by way of explanation dull procedural breaches rather than politicised tampering.

Clearly control over the media and constant changing of electoral legislation represent preferred methods of maintaining the desired multi-party system of elections at the same time as thwarting any danger that power might actually be undermined by opposition forces; much better to manipulate election results way ahead of polling day, and by legal means, than to cheat on the day. Nonetheless, each election is accompanied by accusations of electoral fraud during the voting process. Most famously in the Duma election of December 2011, there were widespread reports of such ham-fisted methods as ballot box stuffing, deliberate miscounting and 'carousel voting' – when busloads of regime supporters travel from polling station to polling station voting at each one. Such was the level of public disaffection that demonstrations occurred across the country, and, most seriously, a series of large demonstrations demanding fair elections took place in Moscow. An element of the authorities' response to such widespread unrest was the installation for future elections of webcams in polling stations across the country. It is now possible on election days in Russia for anyone to login, pick a polling station and watch the voting process as a virtual observer. During the 2016 parliamentary election a number of blatant cases of ballot stuffing came to light in this way, with clips of misbehaving electoral officials posted online and Russia's Central Electoral Commission taking action against the offenders.

What we have described so far – media control, constant changes in electoral laws and various forms of voting manipulation – represents Russia's normalised politics. It is, for the most part, the way Russia's political system runs, with a relatively free opposition presence, diverse voices in the media, but widely understood boundaries beyond which the authorities may step in. Greater difficulties exist for those unwilling or unable to abide by these norms. It is in – to use a political science term – contentious politics, or the politics of the street, that the going gets still tougher. If anything can be seen to have fazed the Putin regime that has dominated Russia so far in the twenty-first century, it is the spectre of popular unrest. In his early years as President, Vladimir Putin observed the Orange Revolution in Ukraine, when the careful plans of his team and their Ukrainian allies surrounding Ukraine's 2004 presidential election were brought down by mass demonstrations in Kiev. That the United States took the side of the 'orange revolutionaries' deepened Russian concern, convincing the Putin regime that the US in particular and the West more generally would not be averse to a similar revolutionary takeover in Moscow.

Revolution is anathema to Russia's current rulers, whose unique selling point to the Russian people has been the offer of stability and who operate as if state power belongs to them almost by right. The 'colour revolutions' on the streets of Belgrade (2000), Tblisi (2003), Bishkek (2005) and Kiev (2004) prompted Russia's authorities to beef up their abilities when it comes to street politics. An early development was the formation, under the guidance of Kremlin ideologue Vladislav Surkov, of the youth organisation Nashi – which translates as 'Ours' – that combined various state-sponsored opportunities for personal development via summer camps and career-related activities, with the creation of networks of young people prepared to stand up for Russia's leadership and its policies in the contentious politics of the street. Nashi served some purpose for a while, as it demonstrated a degree of popular support for the authorities among the younger generation and provided deniability for the state with regard to the more controversial accusations made against its membership. A cyber-attack against Estonian internet sites following the removal of a monument to Soviet soldiers from its prominent place in Estonia's capital city, Tallin, was attributed to Nashi activists. So too was the 'psychological harassment' of British ambassador Tony Brenton, who endured months in which his residence was picketed, his car followed and many of his speeches interrupted by hecklers. The deniability of distance, however, creates its own problems too. In 2009, police detained a number of Nashi activists involved in a protest against the excessive bonuses awarded to bankers. A couple of years later, the documentary film *Putin's Kiss*, directed by Danish filmmaker Lise Birk Pedersen, focused on the growing disillusionment of prominent Nashi activist Masha Drokova with the movement. In 2014, still in her mid-twenties, Drokova emigrated to the United States, where she is now an investor in Silicon Valley. A *Wall Street Journal* profile of Ms Drokova in 2017 reported her as having 'lost count' of the number of times that she had met with Vladimir Putin.

More recent years have seen the Russian state move on from the deniability but unreliability of Nashi and adopt the less subtle and more traditional approach of using police and courts. The series of large-scale anti-regime demonstrations in Moscow during the election season of 2011–2012 culminated in police action against demonstrators on Bolotnaya Square and what Amnesty International termed the 'hideous injustice' of the prosecution, fining and imprisonment of dozens of people caught up – many in a somewhat arbitrary fashion – in the clashes of that day. Fairly standard practice when dealing with large-scale demonstrations in contemporary Russia has been for the police to round up a large number of demonstrators and hold them for a day or two before releasing them. After the anti-corruption demonstrations in Moscow in spring 2017, hundreds were treated in this way, with a few facing criminal charges for violence and receiving custodial sentences of a year or so as a result.

Another tactic used by Russia's authorities in order to prevent potential opposition to the regime, while insisting that it is operating within the legal parameters of a democratic state, is simply to introduce laws that work against political opponents. Given that the Russian state insists that it holds to the democratic requirements of its constitution – in other words it requires a reason for these laws other than 'to clamp down on the opposition' – a favoured justification for them is national security. Russia is not alone in in the world when it comes to justifying potential human rights restrictions on the grounds of national security, but unlike governments in democratic states that might sometimes struggle to get such legislation through parliament, the Russian Duma does not vote against the executive. In 2012 a law was introduced in Russia that requires non-governmental organisations receiving donations from abroad and engaging in 'political activity' to declare this fact using the term 'foreign agent'. The idea is to imply that such organisations are unpatriotic and in the pay of foreign governments, although political activity is a loose term with potentially wide application; and funding from abroad need not of course have any root in foreign government activity. In June 2017, in response to the Navalny video accusing Dmitry Medvedev of corruption and growing public anger at corrupt officialdom, a law was passed to 'protect the personal data' of state officials and their families, justified as a security precaution in case of foreign interference but now sitting on the statute book as a threat to those – including anti-corruption campaigners – who would reveal such information.

PROTEST AS ART

In November 2013, a 29-year-old performance artist from St Petersburg, Petr Pavlensky, travelled into the centre of Moscow. Like many visitors to Russia's capital, he made his way to Red Square. In front of Lenin's mausoleum on a cold and wet day, he stripped naked, sat down on the ground and nailed his scrotum to the cobbles. There he remained for a while as a one-man protest on Russia's annual Police Day against the apathy and fatalism of Russian society. Not that Red Square is unused to radical protest. The previous winter, in January 2012, eight young women, dressed in brightly coloured leggings, balaclavas and dresses, clambered up onto the large stone platform situated at the south end of the square just outside St Basil's Cathedral. This was the political protest band Pussy Riot. There – on a snowy Red Square, replete with guitars, amplifiers, smoke flares and a clenched fist banner – they belted out a song the title of which could be roughly translated as 'Riot in Russia (Putin has pissed himself)'.

Pavlensky and Pussy Riot made their protests against the Putin regime in ways that were radical in both the artistic and the political sense. Some members of Pussy Riot had been part of a radical art collective Voina which had specialised in uncompromising protest actions including cat throwing, painting a penis on a drawbridge in central St Petersburg and holding an orgy in a Moscow museum. Pussy Riot made international headlines in 2012 when they were arrested after performing a protest song in the Cathedral of Christ the Saviour in Moscow. Their trial revealed something of the unfairness of Russia's judicial system, not only in some of the rather bizarre rulings of the judge, but also in the perfectly standard Russian practice of keeping the accused in cages in the courtroom, treating them as guilty before the verdict.

In protest at the imprisonment of the Pussy Riot activists, Petr Pavlensky stood outside St Isaac's Cathedral in St Petersburg, having sewed his mouth shut as a protest against the silencing of their voice. He held a banner in his hand comparing Pussy Riot's performance in the Cathedral of Christ the Saviour – which had sought to expose corrupt links between the Russian Orthodox Church and the Kremlin – with the biblical account of Jesus overturning the tables of the moneylenders in the temple in Jerusalem. Pavlensky's later protests include being wrapped up naked in barbed wire, slicing off his earlobe with a chef's knife and setting fire to the front door of the Lubyanka building, which is notorious as the headquarters of the KGB in the Soviet era and now the home of Russia's FSB.

The radical nature of such protests is as much to do with their politics as their form. Pussy Riot and Pavlensky are not Western liberals looking for a little more democracy and supporting the free market. Their stance is more akin to the radical activists of their generation that exist in the West as well as in Russia. The treatment of Pussy Riot made headlines and drew widespread condemnation from Western observers, but opinion polls in Russia showed that a majority thought the protests had crossed the boundary of offence and that some prison term at least was justified. The three Pussy Riot members who ended up in prison colonies were released before their sentences ended, but not before one of them – Nadezhda Tolokonnikova – had done much to publicise the appalling conditions and treatment of prisoners in the Russian penal system. In 2017, Pavlensky, his wife and their two children were granted political asylum in France, having been threatened with what they saw as malicious and unwarranted prosecution in Russia.

CASUAL REPRESSION: THE CASE OF ILDAR DADIN

In the summer of 2014, a 32-year-old man from the Moscow region by the name of Ildar Dadin took an A3-sized piece of card and on it in black pen wrote: 'Putin – the downfall of Russia'. Dadin travelled into the centre of Moscow, where he stood in front of a statue of the Second World War military leader Marshall Zhukov that stands near the northern entrance to Red Square and adjacent to the Kremlin walls. He held his home-made sign above his head, in a one-man peaceful protest. By the end of the following year, Ildar Dadin had been sentenced to three years in prison; three years for this and other similar quiet and non-violent expressions of his opinion concerning the people with power in Russia. He served the first few months of his sentence in a Moscow prison before being transferred to a penal colony in northern Karelia. After several weeks there he wrote a letter to his wife, detailing regular beatings, being hung up by his handcuffs, stripped and threatened with rape. Dadin's wife – au fait with the tools of Russian dissidents and in possession of good legal contacts and the intelligence, knowledge and bravery to create a media storm – publicised his case in Russia and abroad. The authorities moved fairly swiftly to transfer him, though even then there was a hiatus of a week or more when she did not know where he was, and the hashtag 'Where is Ildar Dadin?' trended on Russian social media. At the highest level, President Putin's well-known press spokesman Dmitry Peskov promised that Dadin's plight would receive the closest attention and be made known to the President. By the end of February 2017, Dadin had been released on the orders of Russia's Supreme Court.

As is apparent in the Putin regime's response to mass demonstrations against the country's rulers in 2012 and 2017, the coercive capacity of the police and the prison system is employed when deemed necessary. Its nature varies from case to case. As far as the most high-profile opposition figures are concerned, political decisions appear to be made with regard to their treatment. Adjustments to the sentencing of Alexei Navalny in 2012, the presidential pardon for Mikhail Khodorkovsky in 2013 and the early release of the Pussy Riot activists all fall into this category. Less well-known oppositionists who get caught up in the regime's response can find themselves trapped on the conveyor belt of Russia's relentless and brutal judicial and penal systems. Conviction rates in Russia are stunningly high. To be brought to court is effectively to be found guilty in the overwhelming majority of cases. Once in prison, those convicted can be subject to overcrowding, disease, casual brutality and – as made plain in a number of cases exposed online in recent years – torture.

The case of Ildar Dadin sits between these two extremes. Dadin does not campaign for political power or engage in the world of business. When sentenced, he was not a well-known figure, but his conviction was controversial as he became the first person to be convicted under a law the constitutionality of which was queried by the Presidential Human Rights Council and Russia's then human rights ombudsman, Ella Pamfilova. Despite the Russian Constitution's guarantee of freedom of assembly and the rights of citizens to hold meetings, demonstrations, pickets and so on, a new article of the Criminal Code was introduced in 2014 making it illegal to take part in more than two unsanctioned events within 180 days. Dadin's harmless one-person protests fell foul of this new ruling, and fed him into the brutality of Russia's penal system. Although clearly a political prisoner in the sense that he was imprisoned for political protest, it seems that the inhuman treatment meted out to him was relatively standard fare in the particular colony where he was sent, although it was intensified when he refused to readily submit. According to the testimony of his wife, as set out in an interview with a Russian website while he was still in prison but after his case had received public attention, the prison authorities

continue to beat people in exactly the same way, he can hear shouts in the mornings. They don't beat him but they put him in a cell for the ultra-violent and he's in there with a guy who's genuinely crazy. They continue to put pressure on him. They still don't feed him.

PROTEST BEYOND POLITICS

Ildar Dadin is a political protester who became a political prisoner, and was subject to the brutal treatment that is too common in Russian prisons. He protested alone and scarcely threatened the regime at all, except as perhaps a potential precursor of other protests. Pussy Riot and Petr Pavlensky are militant in a markedly outspoken way, and although the nature of their protests attracts publicity, they scarcely appeal to the vast mass of 'ordinary Russians' any more than they would to the general public in the United States, the United Kingdom or, indeed, most countries. Despite their ill-treatment and their evident bravery when it comes to protesting against this state and its abuse of power, these individuals remain peripheral to day-to-day politics in Russia. That is not to say, however, that beyond the likes of Dadin, Pavlensky and Pussy Riot Russians are cowed into submission and afraid to raise their voices. On a relatively regular basis, protests take place in Moscow and elsewhere around specific issues. In the spring of 2017, thousands of Muscovites took part in large protests against the city authorities' plan to relocate them as part of a large 'renovation' project. In the months before that, Russia's long-distance lorry drivers engaged in protest actions against road tolls. In both of these cases the protesters not only objected to the actions of the state, but saw them as a means by which corrupt officials sought to make money.

The protests of Muscovites against forced state acquisition of property, or of long-distance lorry drivers against their conditions, do not seek to overthrow the government, remove Putin from power and establish a new system. They demonstrate rather that opposition and protest in Russia represents a varied phenomenon. At the level of high politics, there are the mildly oppositionist in-system parties that offer different programmes from what the ruling regime puts forward, but have little hope of their implementation and – perhaps more to the point – show little drive to change a political process that permanently marginalises them. Oppositionists beyond these groups show more spark and anger, but have less national profile and public support. In moving increasingly away from generalised and somewhat abstract aims, such as democracy and human rights that can be tarred as somehow pro-Western and anti-Russian, and instead focusing their action and ire on regime corruption, the political opponents of the Putin regime have a strong card to play. But having that card does not mean they can easily play it. Their struggle with the ruling regime pits them against a sophisticated opponent, adept at the use of the propaganda of patriotism, a complex of legal means and – when it comes to it – the violence of state power. As is discussed in Chapter Six, for all the genuine popularity of President Putin among Russians, accusations of corruption represent his Achilles heel in terms of public opinion. It is this issue more than any other that might undermine him and his regime if – as it must do in order to succeed – Russia's political opposition is to extend its reach across the country and to stir up anger and action beyond its metropolitan bases. It is to the vast expanse of Russia beyond these bases that the next chapter turns.

CHAPTER FIVE

POLITICS BEYOND MOSCOW

KHOLMANSKIKH AND THE POWER VERTICAL

Igor Kholmanskikh is not a well-known name in the West. That said, he is scarcely a household name in his native Russia, either. But his story reveals much about Russian politics beyond the 'Moscow village' and out into the vast Eurasian expanse of the Russian Federation. Kholmanskikh serves as President Putin's plenipotentiary representative over an area larger than France, Germany, Spain, Great Britain and Ireland combined. That area – the Urals Federal District – sits on the geographical border of Europe and Asia. It stretches from Kazakhstan in the south to the Arctic Sea in the north, and includes among its cities two with populations of over one million: the industrial city of Chelyabinsk, nicknamed Tankograd (tank city) as it churned out thousands of T-34 tanks crucial to the Red Army's victories over the Nazis during the Second World War; and Yekaterinburg, the scene of the murder of Russia's last Tsar and his family by the Communists in 1918, and the home town of Russia's first post-Soviet President, Boris Yeltsin. Igor Kholmanskikh was made a presidential envoy to this vast region in Russia's heartland at the age of forty-two, shortly after President Putin was inaugurated for his third term in May 2012. His rapid elevation to become presidential plenipotentiary to one of only eight Federal Districts is very revealing as to the nature of both Russia's political system and Moscow's control over the regions in what is by some distance the world's largest country.

It would be a misrepresentation to claim Kholmanskikh won his exalted position in a TV talent show, but it's not a million miles from the truth. Igor Kholmanskikh began his working life in the mid-1990s in the famous 'Uralvagonzavod' (literally, Urals Carriage Factory) in the city of Nizhny Tagil, the second largest city in the Sverdlovsk region after Yekaterinburg. The factory had been built in the 1930s during the great Stalinist industrialisation programme, when the totalitarian state was able to subjugate everything to its primary aim of transforming the Soviet Union from a backward and predominantly rural society to a modern, cutting-edge state capable of competing with the capitalist world in both economic and military terms. Much of the factory's initial construction was carried out by 'special settlers', a labour force made up mostly of peasants removed from their land by the collectivisation drive of the early 1930s and sent to build industry and infrastructure in previously undeveloped areas. In the 1960s, both of Kholmanskikh's parents worked in the train- and tank-building factory at a time when to be an industrial worker was to hold one of the most respected and well-paid jobs in the Soviet Union. By the time Igor Kholmanskikh followed his parents into the factory, however, the Soviet Union no longer existed. Its socialist, planned economy had given way almost overnight to a chaotic, uncontrolled and under-legislated form of capitalism. The great industrial towns of the Urals came to form what was known as Russia's 'rust belt', as living standards and life expectancy plummeted, along with the international standing of what had only a few years earlier been a global superpower.

Wind forward a few years to the beginning of the new millennium, and the arrival of President Putin in office brought about a strengthening of federal state control over the regions, and coincided with almost a decade of high oil prices and resultant economic growth. In December 2009, Vladimir Putin, during his four-year prime ministerial interlude of 2008 to 2012, made a beneficent visit to Uralvagonzavod. As well as observing the construction of T-90 tanks in fulfilment of an export order from India, he announced that his government would provide the company – still majority-owned by the state – with an additional 10 billion rubles (US$330 million) on top of the 8 billion rubles already pledged in debt restructuring and loan guarantees.

The practice of the country's most senior politicians travelling around Russia distributing largesse is common because it works politically, if not always economically. A couple of years after this visit, Putin needed to call in the favour. In late 2011, he had announced his intention to return to the presidency (officially, his intention to seek re-election, but that was indeed a mere technicality). This announcement, followed by widespread accusations of electoral fraud in the parliamentary elections of December that year, sparked mass protests with tens of thousands of anti-regime demonstrators voicing their disapproval on the streets of Moscow. It was then that the televisual talents of Igor Kholmanskikh came to the fore. During Putin's annual marathon televised phone-in on 15 December, Kholmanskikh – by now an assembly workshop foreman in the Uralvagonzavod – was selected to take part in a live link from the factory floor, surrounded by overall-wearing workmates. He delivered his lines well.

> You came to help us in difficult times, Vladimir Vladimirovich ... stability is very dear to us, we don't want to go backwards. So, about these demonstrations; if our police force don't know how to deal with them, or if they can't cope, then me and the boys are ready to come down there ourselves and, er, defend our stability.

Cue warm applause from the studio audience and a wry smile from Putin. The scripted message was clear. Out there, in real Russia, where real people do real jobs, there is little sympathy for airy-fairy talk about democracy and election fraud and human rights. During the 2009 prime ministerial visit, slogans had been posted on the streets proclaiming 'Military production: the work of a real man', and 'The stronger we are, the stronger Russia is'. This was Russia beyond Moscow. These were the people to whom Putin was increasingly looking for support.

Come May 2012, when his re-election to the presidency had been confirmed, President Putin wasted no time in signalling his domestic third-term priorities. After a leader comes to power in Russia, two 'first visits' traditionally have symbolic significance: those are the first trip abroad and the first domestic visit beyond the capital. Just as at the commencement of his previous two terms in office, Putin's first foreign trips in his third term followed the pattern of visiting a fellow European post-Soviet state (in 2012, Belarus) followed by a Western European country (this time, France). Before both of these, however, his emblematic first visit outside the capital was to the Uralvagonzavod in Nizhny Tagil, the defence industry stronghold in Russia's industrial heart, from where the workers had offered to travel to Moscow in order to defend their President from ideologically motivated and ungrateful protesters. This trip sent all of the right signals as to the returning President's priorities.

In order to hammer the message home, President Putin followed his factory visit up a few days later by formally appointing workshop manager Igor Kholmanskikh to the high-level position of presidential plenipotentiary representative to the Urals Federal District. Kholmanskikh was joining illustrious company, as he took his place alongside the other presidential representatives to Russia's Federal Districts, men who had been governors, Chief Prosecutors, State

Ministers, Deputy Head of the Presidential Administration, Interior Forces Commander and a senior FSB officer.

Kholmanskikh's story reveals much about the politics of Russia's regions. The distaste that he and his fellow workers expressed for political demonstrations in Moscow reflects a common attitude in Russia's provinces. It is an attitude shared both by those who support the ruling regime and by those who tend to vote for the Communists or for Zhirinovsky's nationalist and obscurantist Liberal Democratic Party of Russia. Surveys show that outside the capitals of Moscow and St Petersburg, people are less concerned with the more abstract conceptualisations of how Russia should be ruled, and prioritise instead the efficacy of governance as it relates to everyday needs. The visits by Putin to Uralvagonzavod illustrate a mode of engagement that, as Chapter Three sets out, has become known as 'manual control', whereby local issues are as likely to be dealt with by the personal inter-vention of members of the federal hierarchy as by their own regional executives, particularly when it can be exploited for some wider political purpose. The surprise elevation of Kholmanskikh to so senior a position reinforced the inten-tion behind the introduction of the extra-constitutional role of presidential plenipotentiary by the newly elected President Putin in 2000: namely, to demonstrate that the Kremlin's writ runs across all of Russia. From the very first month of his presidency, Putin worked to establish what he called a 'power vertical', which is an institutional arrangement with presidential power at the top able to transmit its authority down the line to regional and then local authorities across the country.

PUTIN AND THE PROVINCES

Vladimir Putin is a man of the capital cities, and the first leader of Russia, or the Soviet Union, to be such since the fall of the Tsar in 1917. His life in Russia has been based in either Moscow or St Petersburg, though he did spend five years posted as a KGB officer in East Germany in the 1980s. Most of what we hear about Russia takes place in Moscow and St Petersburg. Moscow's Red Square is iconic as a symbol of Russia and of the Soviet Union; pick up any paperback thriller or spy novel with a Russian theme and there's a good chance that the cover will feature some variation of Moscow's centrepiece. Perhaps a silhouetted figure standing in the snow on the edge of the vast square, behind him the unmistakable onion domes of St Basil's Cathedral (officially known as the Cathedral of the Intercession of the Blessed Virgin Mary). Perhaps a more panoramic scene of the Kremlin itself with its towers and gate houses, its palaces and official offices, its soaring red-brick walls with the gleaming cupolas of five cathedrals and churches rising behind them. But these cities are, of course, atypical in Russian terms.

St Petersburg has its own complex and resonant past. Seat of the Communist revolution in 1917 and birthplace and home town of President Putin, it was built on the orders of Peter the Great (1672–1725), the Westernising Tsar, to be a modern European capital for a modern European Russia.

Constructed in straight boulevards lined with neoclassical buildings, St Petersburg from its very foundation marked itself as a city apart. The new Imperial capital rejected the higgledy-piggledy lanes of Moscow's urban districts, just as the Emperor Peter turned his back on what he saw as the backward and Byzantine practices of old Russia. Renamed Leningrad for most of the Soviet era, St Petersburg suffered a brutal siege during the Second World War after being completely encircled by the Nazis from September 1941 to January 1943. Well over half a million citizens died from starvation and disease. In the Piskaryovskoye Memorial Cemetery just to the north-east of the city centre, the bodies of around 420,000 civilian victims of the siege are buried, many in mass graves. Among these victims was a young child by the name of Viktor Spiridonovich Putin, who died of diphtheria during the siege. Viktor was one of the two brothers of Vladimir Putin, both of whom died well before the future President was born in October 1952 in Leningrad.

Putin is very much a native of Leningrad. Born and brought up there with the horrors of war so recent, he trained for a year in Moscow and then between 1985 and 1990 he was posted as a KGB officer to Dresden in Communist East Germany (the German Democratic Republic, GDR). Until 1989, the Brezhnevite Erich Honecker led the GDR's ruling Socialist Unity Party and the Stasi secret police controlled its society, with around one in eight people acting as informants against their fellow citizens. Putin was holed up in one of the most unbendingly old-style Communist states, while his compatriots at home experienced the rapid liberalisation of the Gorbachev years. Back in the Soviet Union, reformist voices questioned the old, accepted totalitarian truths and began to seize both headlines and power.

As the old Communist world collapsed, Putin returned to Leningrad – then on the brink of being renamed St Petersburg – to cut his political teeth working as a deputy to his former professor and now reformist mayor of the city, Anatoly Sobchak. Many of his close political colleagues – including future President Dmitry Medvedev – followed him from St Petersburg to Moscow in the 1990s, in keeping with the Russian political tradition of senior figures having a *khvost*, or tail, of personnel accompanying them on their rise to power. While causal links between past experience and present politics ought not to be overstated, Vladimir Putin's policies towards Russia's regions reflect a preference for control from the capital and a degree of uniformity across the country.

FORMING A FEDERATION

Russia is formally a federation. Aping the US Constitution, Russia's constitution begins: 'We, the multinational peoples of the Russian Federation...' The first article proper of the Russian Constitution asserts that 'the names "Russian Federation" and "Russia" shall be equal'. But the balance between central (federal) and regional government in Russia has swung too far in both directions since the collapse of the Soviet Union, and has struggled to settle on a satisfactory equilibrium. Before Vladimir Putin became President in 2000, the constitutional powers granted to the centre frequently foundered on the autonomous ambitions of regional leaders, many of whom exercised their influence over vast territories thousands of miles and several time zones away from Moscow. Driven by diverse factors – ethnic, kleptocratic and vain – regional leaders in the 1990s lived through auspicious times for the assertion of self-government. At the beginning of that decade, the formidable Soviet state had fallen victim to the drive for regional self-rule. If Turkmenistan and Kyrgyzstan could be independent countries, then why could the Republic of Tatarstan – situated within Russia – not at least enjoy de facto independence, if not even de jure? In any case, the newly formed Russian state under President Yeltsin was no formidable superpower. It had only just regained its own independence from the Soviet Union under the leadership of a President who had urged independence-minded republics within Russia – that is, not the other fourteen republics of the Soviet Union that gained independence in 1991 – to 'take as much sovereignty as you can swallow'. Having recklessly advocated such secessionist drives in Tatarstan and Bashkortostan during the heady days of 1990 when he was focused on undermining the authority of Soviet leader Gorbachev, Yeltsin found it difficult to row back from this position once he had become the President of an independent Russia and was seeking to hold it together.

A further spur towards the devolution of power from the centre to the regions during the 1990s was that Russia was a weak state, in the sense that it struggled to do that which a state ought to do. The transition from Communism to capitalism was accompanied not only by economic catastrophe but also by a void in legislation. Tax avoidance was rife. Only a barely functioning fiscal framework existed, and it largely failed when it came to picking much of worth from Russia's economic bones. Municipalities and regions bore the brunt of collapsing welfare provision, deficient healthcare, an inadequate education system and the failure to maintain law and order. Particularly so far as the richer regions were concerned – and 'richer' here is certainly a comparative measure – the idea of collecting taxes and sending sparse funds to Moscow was not attractive. These comparatively stronger regions sought to ensure that when it came to tax collection, regional taxes received priority over federal.

SOME REGIONS ARE MORE EQUAL THAN OTHERS

For much of the 1990s, governance in many of Russia's regions carried on with little more than a nod of acquiescence towards the formal federal hierarchy. During this period the Russian Federation was made up of eighty-nine regions. Constitutionally speaking, Russia's regions are equal in their relationship with the federal centre. But these allegedly equal regions have different titles and differing privileges. On the passing of the Russian Federation's constitution in 1993, most regions – forty-nine at the time – were called *oblasts*. In addition, there were six *krais* (provinces), ten autonomous *okrugs* (districts), one autonomous *oblast* (the Jewish autonomous *oblast*), two cities of federal significance (Moscow and St Petersburg) and twenty-one republics within the Russian Federation. The constitution allowed these republics to have their own republican constitutions, albeit that these were supposed to correspond to the federal constitution. The title 'President' could also be applied to the executive head of a republic, since Russia's republics had constitutions and Presidents, while all the other regions had charters and governors.

Ignoring the federal constitution and the legal hierarchy according to which the new Russian state was established, more than half of the constitutions and charters of Russia's regions contradicted the federal constitution during the 1990s. Bashkortostan's 1993 constitution, for example, declared its supremacy in law and abrogated to itself the right to establish its own foreign policy. Tatarstan's constitution pronounced the republic to be a sovereign state. Nor were such contradictions with the supreme federal law confined merely to declaratory documents such as republican constitutions. About one third of regional laws in Russia during the 1990s failed to conform to legal or constitutional provisions as laid down by the federal authorities. In a logical response to regional declarations of sovereignty, the Russian Federation during Yeltsin's presidency (1991–1999) signed forty-six bilateral treaties with members of that same Federation.

These bilateral treaties brought nuance and flexibility to centre-region relations in Russia during the shaky 1990s, when realistic fears of a further breakup of the Russian state were widespread. They headed off the possibility of intractable impasse by providing an avenue of consultation rather than conflict. Such treaties kept the different parties talking and facilitated a collaborative process for building the new Russian state that amounted – and necessarily so – to more than central diktat. These bilateral treaties temporarily filled the legislative gaps that were inevitable in the short term while a new state with completely new political and economic systems was being built. Nor were the treaties even, as might be imagined, entirely extra-constitutional, since Russia's 1993 constitution stipulated that the means by which power would be divided among the Russian Federation and its subjects included 'other treaties' (Article 11.3). On the other hand, for those seeking to strengthen a unitary state, a series of ad hoc treaties with bespoke provisions for different regions undermined the power of the Russian state and its President. For legal and constitutional experts, bilateral treaties between a federation and members of that federation served to confuse the status of federal law and undermined the authority of the federal constitution that insists on a correspondence of regional legal provisions with those decided at the centre.

REINING IN RUSSIA'S REGIONS

Vladimir Putin is both a proponent of a strong unitary state and, by academic background at least, has a legal mind. The central domestic narrative of his regime during the 2000s was that the 1990s were chaotic and that he has restored strong statehood to Russia. In terms of relations between the centre and the regions, the federal pendulum has swung back from the provinces to Moscow. In today's Russia, there are fewer regions than there were in the 1990s; bilateral treaties between regions and the centre are a thing of the past; presidential plenipotentiaries oversee groups of regions; regional leaders know that their positions depend on the Kremlin; the strategic withholding of tax from the centre by the regions has largely ceased; and the leaders of Russia's republics are no longer allowed to hold the title 'President'. There is only one President in Russia these days.

Re-establishing power over the regions was a priority for President Putin from the off. Within days of his inauguration in May 2000, he made his decisive move and hit the heads of the regions with a double whammy that diminished their status at the national level and placed them under robust presidential scrutiny. The opening move came in his first televised address to the nation, when Putin announced that regional leaders could no longer combine that position with a seat in the upper house of Russia's parliament, the Federation Council. After all, he argued, it contradicted the principle of separation of powers for those who wield executive power in their regions to simultaneously be the legislators passing the laws that they themselves have to implement. His less technical and more popular explanation for the move was that these regional bosses had more than enough on their plates running their regions without spending many weeks each year in Moscow as members of the federal parliament. The constitutional provision that requires members of the

Federation Council to come, one each respectively, from the executive and the legislature of each region remains intact, since it is representatives of these bodies who sit in the upper house of Russia's parliament today.

In his pragmatic way, having removed the status of regional heads as national politicians and scuppered their monthly Moscow get-togethers, Putin threw them a bone a few months later. He issued a decree in September 2000 on the establishment of a State Council, to be made up of regional heads and to meet several times a year under the chairmanship of the President, in order to advise him in his role as the head of state of the Russian Federation. This State Council echoes in its task and title, if not its make-up, the State Council of Imperial Russia that advised the Tsar. It has no constitutional status, nor are its decisions binding on the President. The State Council made an early impression when, in its first meeting, discussion centred on the restoration of the Soviet-era national anthem, albeit with new words. These days the State Council rarely makes the headlines, particularly since it discusses such worthy but somewhat dull issues as infrastructure, road safety and tourism.

The second element of the double whammy against regional leaders in May 2000 also entailed the establishment of institutions that are not mentioned in Russia's constitution. Putin announced that he was creating seven Federal Districts, each one to have its own presidential plenipotentiary representative. In 2010, with the creation of the North Caucasus Federal District, these seven districts became eight.

The presidential representatives – one of whom Igor Khol-manskikh was to become a dozen years later – had the task of 'guaranteeing the realisation of the constitutional powers of the head of state' in the regions within each Federal District. They report directly to the President and sit on the Security Council, and the majority of those appointed to these roles over the years have had a military or security forces background. Like the State Council, their role and profile have diminished over time. At first the task was clear: to bring regional laws and constitutions into line with federal legislation. This was successfully accomplished, for the most part through working with and not against regional authorities. In today's Russia, however, the presidential plenipotentiaries have a less clear role. Regional heads tend to marry effective working relations at the federal level with the position of regional linchpin at the nexus of business-political-popular activities.

The selection of governors themselves has, like much policy in relation to regions, seen a number of changes in approach in the post-Soviet years. Regional heads were initially elected. After the terrorist atrocity at Beslan school in 2004, however, President Putin – in what seemed to be a rather crass non sequitur following the death of over 300 people, almost 200 of whom were children – declared a key lesson from this tragedy to be that Russia required a radical institutional restructuring in order to strengthen its unity. The major plank of this restructuring was for the heads of regional executives to be appointed by the President from then on. In this way, Vladimir Putin, and, between 2008 and 2012, Dmitry Medvedev, could far more effectively ensure loyalty and obedience from those leading the Russian Federation's subjects. In 2011, during a period of anti-regime demonstrations, President Medvedev announced the restoration of gubernatorial elections. This movement back to an apparently democratic selection of regional leaders has some strings attached, known respectively as the presidential filter and the municipal filter. The presidential filter works by the President consulting with political parties as to which candidates they might field. In Russia's political system, consultation with the President amounts to an informal veto power that can be used by the Kremlin in the case of unwanted candidacies. The municipal filter involves all candidates being required to obtain the approval of a proportion (around 10 per cent) of local deputies and municipal leaders in their region. Finally a law of 2013 allows regional legislatures to request that the President appoints the governor rather than the people of the region doing so through an electoral process.

By 2014, the Russian Federation was made up of eighty-five regions according to its own definition, although the vast majority of states do not recognise Russia's acceptance of Crimea into the Federation in March of that year. Between 2005 and 2008, six autonomous *okrugs* held referendums in which they agreed to merge with their surrounding regions, thereby reducing eighty-nine regions to eighty-three. When Crimea was annexed in 2014, two more regions were added to the Russian Federation. Official and popular euphoria at the addition of this territory to the list of federal subjects no doubt accounts for the somewhat artificially boosted status of the two new regions added. Crimea itself received the status of Republic, despite this previously having been reserved for ethnic homelands whose name is taken from the titular ethnic group. The capital of Crimea, Simferopol, joined Moscow and St Petersburg to become one of only three 'cities of federal importance' and a subject of the Russian Federation in its own right with two seats in the Federation Council. Were Simferopol to be included in a list of Russian cities by population, it would not make the top fifty.

PROVINCIAL PERSONNEL AND THE PUTIN TEAM

In Russian and Soviet political history – as in the United States – running a region has served for several politicians as a form of apprenticeship ahead of national leadership. Mikhail Gorbachev (leader of the Soviet Union between 1985 and 1991) spent his early career in his native Stavropol region, serving as first secretary there for a decade in the 1970s before moving to Moscow. Russia's first post-Soviet President, Boris Yeltsin, similarly spent ten years as Communist party boss in Sverdlovsk ahead of coming to the capital. Neither President Putin nor President Medvedev have had such provincial backgrounds, and in the opening decades of this century there has been a tendency for senior political positions to go to those with long-standing connections to the President. That tendency is not a rule. Focused expertise and experience matters in relevant positions; for example,

Foreign Minister Sergei Lavrov is one of the world's most experienced international politicians, having joined the Soviet Foreign Ministry in the early 1970s and worked his way up. On occasion, competent regional politicians are still brought to Moscow to join the governing team. The Mayor of Moscow, Sergei Sobyanin, entered national politics in 2005, when President Putin identified the then governor of the Tyumen region in Siberia as loyal and competent, and surprised political commentators by bringing this outsider into his team in the powerful position of Head of the Presidential Administration.

When a regime remains in power without serious challenge or threat for many years, as the Putin regime has and as the Soviet regime did in the twentieth century, analysts devote inordinate attention to personnel changes below the apex of power. It's understandable. With nothing moving when it comes to the top job and stability being the President's watchword – or stagnation, as critics would have it – any personnel movement is more interesting than none. And in any case, the longer Putin remains in power, then by definition, the nearer we are to the end of his presidency. In the days of the Soviet Union, analysts who spent their time poring over the minutiae of lower level personnel shifts in order to discern who was up and who was down gained the title 'kremlinologists'. Who stood next to whom atop Lenin's Mausoleum for the May Day parade on Red Square was deemed indicative of a coming or fading political career. As the increasing longevity of the Putin presidency is matched by its opacity, the art of Kremlinology has been making a comeback. Regional reshuffles provide plenty of scope for reading the political runes.

In the autumn of 2016, a case arose that bamboozled even the most astute and well-connected followers of Russia's regional politics: namely, a presidential decree appointed thirty-year-old Anton Andreevich Alikhanov as the acting governor of Kaliningrad *oblast*. Kaliningrad is no ordinary Russian region. Geographically it is Russia's most westerly territory, being an exclave that borders Poland to the south and Lithuania to the east, and provides the main base for the Russian Navy's strategically important Baltic fleet. Politically Kaliningrad has proved problematic in recent years. In January 2010, Russia's largest anti-government protests in a decade took place there. Sparked by transport and utility price increases, a demonstration brought more than 10,000 people onto the streets to be addressed by opposition figures, including former Deputy Prime Minister and regional governor, the late Boris Nemtsov, who had flown in from Moscow. Demonstrators called for the dismissal of Kaliningrad's governor, Georgy Boos, and the restoration of gubernatorial elections. Following the logic of these two demands, they called, too, for the resignation of then Prime Minister Putin, who, during his previous presidential term, had both abolished the direct election of governors and subsequently appointed Boos to his gubernatorial position. The demonstrators got their immediate and politically easiest demand, when Boos was ousted from his post. A United

Russia party spokesman noted that while Boos might have survived in most other regions, Kaliningrad was a special case. President Medvedev commented that regional leaders need the support of the population.

The appointment of thirty-year-old Alikhanov in October 2016 to the (initially acting) gubernatorial post of this significant region puzzled observers, not simply because of the new incumbent's youthfulness, but because journalists could dig up no dirt on the fresh-faced new boss. The standard expectation among watchers of Russian politics would be that so rapid a rise stems from its recipient being the son of some influential figure, or perhaps having 'useful' business connections, or maybe benefiting from a power struggle between competing factions in Moscow. When it came to Alikhanov's predecessor, things had been much more straightforward. Yevgeny Zinichev had spent many years in the Federal Security Guard Service and had been part of President Putin's personal escort. He fitted a pattern – close links with the President, loyal and with a security forces background. Sometimes, however, even in Putin's Russia, such credentials do not suffice. He didn't appear to make the transition to public life well, and lasted only a few months in post before returning to Moscow. Zinichev's appointment earlier in 2016 had been of a piece with other regional appointments that year; Alexey Dyumin, another former bodyguard, took over in the Tula region in February 2016 and rapidly began to be tipped as a future President; Dmitry Mironov, who was appointed to the governor's seat in Yaroslavl *oblast* in July, had a typical *siloviki* (security forces) background, ex-KGB, ex-Ministry of Interior. Alikhanov, on the other hand, has an academic background in tax law and, before being moved to Kaliningrad, had racked up a mere five years as a Moscow-based civil servant.

FROM CONNECTIONS TO COMPETENCE

Why would such an unknown and junior figure be fast-tracked in this way? The rather dull reason for this rapid advancement would appear to be competence. The Alikhanov appointment fits into a wider narrative in today's Russia surrounding 'the rise of the technocrats' and the de-politicisation of regional politics. After years of trying different methods, Russia's federal government has made progress in introducing rating systems to measure the efficacy of regional governance. Being a former judo partner or hockey buddy of the President might still have influence, but that's not one of the factors on the ratings list. Instead, and appropriately enough, regional administrations are judged by criteria such as economic performance, fiscal efficiency, provision of social goods, satisfaction of the population, law and order and so on. Speaking in December 2016, Vladimir Putin enthused about the injection of new blood into Russia's regional élite, emphasising that these are young, energetic individuals chosen because they have demonstrated in their careers an ability to cope with the practical tasks and duties demanded of a governor.

The technocratic trend continued in the early months of 2017: 37-year-old Maksim Reshetnikov returned to his native region as governor of Perm Krai, after half a dozen years learning the governance trade in the Moscow city administration; forty-year-old former Deputy Minister of Transport Alexey Tsydenov was appointed head of the Republic of Buryatia; and 37-year-old Andrei Nikitin, a businessman with an MBA from the Stockholm School of Economics, was put in charge of the Novgorod *oblast*, having caught the attention of President Putin through his company's innovative road-building projects. With Putin himself constitutionally eligible – by means of a fourth term in office – of remaining as President until 2024, it is not too fanciful to suppose that the regime may be scouting out or training up potential successors from among a cadre of regional leaders in a context where competence matters more than contacts, performance more than politics. In terms of effective governance, a return to the practice, common in other large states and in Soviet history, of budding national leaders proving their worth on a smaller regional scale might prove beneficial to the Russian people.

When it comes to interpreting regional reshuffles, pragmatic patronage is key. The technocratic trend represents a rising tendency, but with eighty-five regions making up the Russian Federation, there exists plenty of room too for considerations other than competence to be taken into account. Balancing factions, rewarding close colleagues, allowing independent figures to respond to specific regional factors and even throwing the occasional gubernatorial bone to the Communist Party and the Liberal Democratic Party of Russia – scope remains for all of these.

THE CHECHEN EXCEPTION

Of all the specific regional factors to be taken account of in Russia's regional politics today, the most well-known and politically difficult are to be found in Chechnya. Although superficially similar, the appointment by President Putin in 2016 of the thirty-year-old Anton Alikhanov as acting head of the historically and politically distinctive Kaliningrad region at the geographical edge of Russia differs dramatically from the appointment by President Putin in 2007 of the thirty-year-old Ramzan Kadyrov as acting head of the historically and politically distinctive Chechen Republic at the geographical edge of Russia.

Ramzan Kadyrov's rise to the top of Chechen politics stemmed from more elemental factors than technocratic competence. His story is one of violence, death, war, passion, pride, grief, love, money, celebrity, family, revenge and devotion. Kadyrov's life was transformed on 9 May 2004 when a bomb exploded at the main stadium of the Chechen capital, Grozny, during the annual Victory Day parade, killing his father, Akhmad Kadyrov, the President of Chechnya. Ramzan Kadyrov was twenty-seven years old at the time. He was his father's second son, and had been close to him through his rise from rebel militia commander fighting the Russian forces in the first Chechen war (1994–1996) to head of the republic, appointed by Putin in September 2000 and formally elected President of Chechnya in 2003. In the clan-based politics of Chechnya, the assassination of Akhmad Kadyrov immediately turned the attention onto his sons as potential successors. Ramzan's elder brother, Zelimkhan Kadyrov, also grief-stricken and having suffered severe injuries in a car accident some months earlier, died of a reported heart attack just three weeks after his father's death. In such tragic circumstances, however, Ramzan Kadyrov's path to the presidency opened up.

The fact that it was not until 2007 that he took on the presidency of his republic illustrates the motif of clashing cultures central to Chechnya's place in the Russian Federation. While the blood-ties of clan politics made Ramzan the obvious successor to his father, the formality of a law-based Russian political system put two obstacles in the way. First, according to the Chechen Constitution, its President must be at least thirty years old. Second, President Putin's decision, following the Beslan atrocity in 2004, to replace elections for regional leaders with direct presidential appointments meant that the presidency of Chechnya was now formally in his gift. These two potential obstacles were overcome by, respectively, patience and a close relationship between Putin and Ramzan Kadyrov. It appears that from the assassination of the elder Kadyrov in May 2004 onwards, the relationship between Vladimir Putin and Ramzan Kadyrov has reflected that between a father and his son. Putin told Chechen television in 2011 that he considered Ramzan to be like a son to him. Kadyrov in his turn has been quoted as saying that he owes his life to President Putin and is devoted to him. Once Ramzan Kadyrov had turned thirty, Putin issued a decree appointing him President of Chechnya.

Chechnya – or the Chechen Republic – is situated in the far south-east of Europe if we are to take the Caucasus Mountains to be Europe's southern border. The politics of Chechnya in particular, and of the wider North Caucasus region more generally, represent, however, a sort of domestic politics that is alien to most European states. Their distinctive nature is seen within regional political life and in relation to Chechnya's place in Russia. There have been two brutal wars fought to maintain Moscow's control over the region. From the perspective of the Chechen side, the first war (1994–1996) had a predominantly separatist character. The second war – officially fought between 1999 and 2000, though with an insurgency phase lasting for much of the first decade of this century – took on a more Islamist character, overlapping with wider international conflicts. From the perspective of the Russian side – and indeed of international law – these were not wars of expansion or invasion on the part of Russia, but civil wars aimed at maintaining the integrity of the Russian state in the face of violent separatism.

TERRORISM IN RUSSIA – THE CHECHEN CONNECTION

In this age in which terrorism plays so formative a role in domestic and international politics across the world, we in the West are too familiar with the devastating impact of terrorist activity on a nation's psyche. 9/11 in the United States, 7/7 in London, Madrid, Utøya, Paris, Brussels, Munich, Stockholm, Manchester – these represent but a few of the attacks that have murdered thousands, devastated the lives of many more and shaped political attitudes and actions as nations and their governments have sought appropriate responses. Comparisons are odious, and it is no part of the argument here to weigh levels of suffering and atrocity one against another. Suffice to say that appalling acts of terror have afflicted Russia and its people with remarkable regularity and ferocity during the Putin era, and that the vast majority of these have their roots within Russia itself – and, more specifically, within the Chechen Republic.

Within weeks of President Boris Yeltsin appointing Vladimir Putin Prime Minister in August 1999, Chechen forces numbering roughly 2,000 troops began an incursion into neighbouring Dagestan, a republic within the Russian Federation. Later that week, a bomb went off in Moscow's newly constructed Manezh shopping mall a few hundred metres from the Kremlin. As Russian Interior Ministry troops fought back in Dagestan, a car bomb destroyed an apartment block in the town of Buynaksk, killing more than sixty residents. Apartment bombings followed in Moscow, with two blocks destroyed in one week as their residents slept. More than 200 people were killed, twice that number injured, and Moscow's inhabitants were put on high alert. Most Muscovites live in high-rise blocks and for a week or so people went to bed each evening wondering if their block would be the next target. A few days after the second Moscow bombing, another block of flats was destroyed by a bomb, this time in the city of Volgodonsk in southern Russia, causing seventeen fatalities. Similar to what happened after

9/11 in the United States, opponents of Russia's ruling regime promoted conspiracy theories seeking to blame elements within the Russian state itself for the bombings. Meanwhile, terrorist attacks continued.

In 2002, about forty Chechen terrorists occupied a theatre in Moscow which was packed for a performance of the musical *Nord-Ost*. After a stand-off of more than two days, with terrified theatre-goers trapped with neither food nor sanitation, the terrorists began shooting hostages. Russian Special Forces pumped gas into the theatre to disable the terrorists and then stormed the building. All of the terrorists were killed, but adverse reactions to the gas killed up to 130 hostages. The next year saw a female suicide bomber blow herself up in the entrance queue at a Moscow rock festival, murdering twenty festival-goers. A few months later, a suicide attack outside the National Hotel opposite the Kremlin killed five people. Altogether, a total of around 300 victims were killed in suspected Chechen attacks in 2003. In 2004, as well as the attack that killed Akhmad Kadyrov, two major bombing attacks on the Moscow metro took the lives of over fifty people and wounded hundreds; two domestic passenger flights were blown up in August, killing all on board; and two car bombs were detonated in the city of Voronezh. Then, in September 2004, the horror of the Beslan atrocity saw hundreds of children, celebrating their return to school, taken hostage by armed Chechen fighters, tortured over three days and then killed in the mayhem surrounding a rescue attempt.

In April 2017, a report by the European Court of Human

Rights (ECHR) into Russia's actions surrounding the 2004 Beslan tragedy blamed poor tactics and implementation on the part of the rescuers for many deaths, just as an ECHR report in 2011 criticised Russian security forces' response to the 2002 theatre siege. The brutality of the conduct of the two Chechen wars no doubt brutalised in turn Chechen terrorists. As with almost all acts of terror across the world, there are contextual circumstances that can complicate a simple narrative. Nonetheless, the fact remains that the experience of terror of the Russian people and state has corresponded, at the least, to that of many Western states this century.

Any one of the attacks noted in the preceding paragraph would dominate the media, public discussion and policymaking in any country. And that paragraph by no means covers the full litany of terror. Twice, in 2007 and 2009, the main express train from Moscow to St Petersburg was bombed, killing over fifty people in total. The Moscow metro was targeted again by suicide bombers in 2010, with at least forty dead. Thirty-seven were murdered in a bomb blast at Moscow's Domodedovo airport in 2011. Suicide attacks on public transport in the city of Volgograd (formerly Stalingrad) in 2013 killed thirty-four people. The attackers were claimed to be members of the Caucasus Emirate, a militant Russian Islamist group that stems partly from Chechen Islamist movements and sought to establish an Islamic emirate in the North Caucasus region of Russia. The same group launched attacks in the Chechen capital, Grozny, in 2014. The following year, a Russian passenger plane was blown up over Egypt's Sinai peninsula by a bomb on board, killing its 224 passengers and crew. The Islamic State group claimed responsibility. In April 2017, two bombs were planted on the St Petersburg metro system; one was found and safely destroyed, the other killed fifteen people. Even this list ignores the multiple acts of violence that killed hundreds – mainly Islamist fighters and Russian security forces – in the North Caucasus area between around 2009 and 2013, facilitated by the increased networking of Russian Islamist groups with wider militant Islamist movements; many of the fighters involved joined the conflict in Syria. When Islamic State in Syria declines, any of these fighters who remain alive may well return to Russian territory.

RAMZAN KADYROV'S RULES

This diversion to outline the terrorist acts in Russia provides violent context to the relationship between Putin and Kadyrov and between Moscow and Chechnya. After a decade and a half of brutal conflict, by the mid-2000s Putin's plan for peace was clear. Like a medieval monarch dealing with a vassal state, Russia's President wanted a reliably loyal subject who would keep order in Chechnya – someone who would keep Chechnya in the Russian Federation and follow Moscow's lead on the issues that matter to Moscow. In return, Moscow would effectively treat Chechnya as a special case in many respects – Kadyrov would have carte blanche in terms of ruling the region and operating in ways beyond the norm across most of Russia. For the most part, this is how things are managed in respect of this very particular member of the Russian Federation. Even the distinctive appearance of its leader sets it apart from Russia's other regions, as the bearded Kadyrov appears in formal settings and meetings wearing tracksuits or casual jackets. When it comes to 'traditional' – for which read 'socially conservative' at best – attitudes towards homosexuals, women, the rights of husbands over their wives and so on, then Kadyrov roams free with his assertions and counsel. When it comes to enjoying the perquisites of power, such as personal wealth being used to bring an array of Hollywood stars to his birthday party, then that appears to be accepted behaviour. When it comes to national elections, Chechnya habitually delivers a vote of more than 95 per cent for the candidate of Russia's ruling regime. Don't question the democracy: feel the loyalty. Kadyrov has been particularly strong on personal loyalty to Putin. In response to EU sanctions against Russia introduced after the annexation of Crimea in 2014, he brought in his own sanctions, including banning President Obama, European Commission President José Manuel Barroso, EU foreign policy commissioner Catherine Ashton and European Council chief Herman van Rompuy from travelling to Chechnya.

Beyond these documented aspects of Kadyrov's rule in Chechnya, a series of serious allegations about the behaviour of his security forces in the region have been made in the media and by human rights groups. In April 2017, the liberal Moscow-based newspaper *Novaya gazeta* began publishing reports of gay men being arrested and tortured in

Chechnya, with at least three said to have died in the process. According to Amnesty International, accounts from Russia suggested that the actions in Chechnya developed after a Moscow-based LGBT rights group was reported to have applied for permits to stage rallies across Russia, including in Muslim-majority regions. The treatment of homosexual men in Chechnya rapidly became an issue of international significance and was raised at the summit meeting between President Putin and German Chancellor Angela Merkel in May 2017. Problematic also for the Putin regime are those occasions when the violent 'solutions' of a policy that was shaped by brutal conflict during the two Chechen wars appear to move beyond the borders of Chechen territory. The somewhat laissez-faire attitude of the Putin regime to Kadyrov's management of Chechnya does, however, have its limits. Those limits involve ensuring that, for all the blind eyes turned to aspects of his leadership of the Chechen Republic, Kadyrov does not transgress too overtly beyond his fiefdom, and the status of Chechnya as a subject of the Russian Federation remains regularly reinforced.

Aforementioned former Deputy Prime Minister turned leading opposition figure Boris Nemtsov was shot dead on a bridge near the Kremlin in February 2015. The five men found guilty of his murder by a Moscow jury in June 2017 come from Chechnya, though the case remains murky in terms of the motivation and chain of command behind the assassination. The months after Nemtsov's death coincided with an emphasis on the part of Russia's federal authorities that Chechnya cannot exist simply as an independently acting fiefdom, and with a series of press articles musing on whether the model of loyal vassal with behavioural carte blanche in return for delivering stability had outgrown its usefulness. The further back in time were the vicious Chechen wars, the weaker the grounds for turning a blind eye to what might have been excused by the exigencies of conflict. Press reports of a conflict – in terms of rhetoric, at least – between the federal security forces in Moscow and the Chechen authorities flourished into the summer of 2015. They were stoked by Kadyrov's public statement, in response to a specific incident, that should federal officers 'whether from Moscow or Stavropol' appear in Chechnya then Chechen law enforcement officers should shoot to kill. This statement was reportedly met by a formal reminder from the Russian Ministry of the Interior that the chain of command in Chechnya, as in the rest of the Russian Federation, means that the police there answer to the Ministry of the Interior in Moscow.

In January 2016, Kadyrov, whose term as head of the Chechen Republic was due to expire later that year, held a rally in Grozny. An estimated 700,000 people were on the streets, carrying neat pre-prepared banners that either praised Kadyrov and Putin or heaped opprobrium on leaders of Russia's liberal opposition, branding them fifth columnists and friends of America. In September 2016, Kadyrov, with the approval of Putin, was re-elected as head of the Chechen Republic. He received 97.9 per cent of the votes cast; the remaining 2.1 per cent were shared between his three opponents. In a country where authoritarianism often wears a democratic disguise, and the days of almost 100 per cent election results were left behind when the Soviet Union disappeared, Chechnya remains an exception.

CHAPTER SIX

PUBLIC OPINION

WHAT RUSSIANS THINK AND WHETHER IT MATTERS

What do Russians think? On one level that seems a ridiculous question. In 2017, there were about 146 million people living in Russia. We can – and indeed this chapter does – generalise about the collective views of so many individuals, but for almost any opinion expressed, there will be tens of millions of Russian citizens who think differently. Consider for a moment how this 146 million is made up. As in any country, the views of the young are likely to differ from those of the old, with the life-transforming technological advances of recent decades differentiating generations the world over, particularly in terms of access to information and knowledge of a world beyond their own geographical limitations. But the generational experiences of the people of Russia display particularly stark differences that include, but go far beyond, technological progress.

More than a quarter of Russia's population – roughly 40 million people – were born after the collapse of Communism in 1991. Their parents' – or in some cases by now, grandparents' – generation literally lived in a different country: the Soviet Union. There, almost everything was owned and controlled by the state, knowledge of the outside world was limited and censored, and foreign travel lay beyond the dreams of the vast majority of the population because their government wouldn't let them out. Even if we consider just those of Russia's citizens who were born in the post-Soviet years, the early years of around a third of these were the 1990s, a period of economic collapse, the failure of basic state provision in areas such as health and education and widespread existential despair at the state of Russia. Generational differences are not the only ones of significance. Life experience varies also according to economic and geographical factors, as our discussion of attitudes to income differentials and nationalism later in this chapter demonstrates.

Variations in experience and attitude between people of different generations, diverse income levels and a multitude of other distinctions do not diminish the utility of public opinion polling. Indeed, they enhance the richness and fascination of sociological surveys, demonstrating the validity and specificities of generalisations and testing the robustness of conventional assumptions. If then it is indeed worth asking what Russians think, how can we be sure about the answer we get? Can we know what Russians think? Opinion polling as a science did not exist in the Soviet Union until its very end. In 1989, two years before the Soviet Union collapsed, the All-Russia Public Opinion Research Center (VTsIOM), emerged on the scene, run by Yuri Levada. Soviet leader Mikhail Gorbachev (1985–1991) had become known for his policy of *glasnost*; usually translated as openness, the word *glasnost* has the sense, too, of giving people a voice. For decades, the Soviet Union – for all its ideological positioning as a 'state of all the people' – had told its citizens what was right and what was to be done, rather than asking them for their views. All of a sudden, in line with *glasnost*, opinion pollsters began to find out what the people thought. The All-Russia Public Opinion Research Center flourished into the post-Soviet era, gaining a reputation for independence, accuracy and a willingness to ask all sorts of questions, however sensitive. As the power of the Russian state was restored under Vladimir Putin from 2000 onwards, so the independence of the All-Russia Public Opinion Research Center came under threat. Polling pioneer Yuri Levada left to form his own public opinion agency, the Levada Center, in 2003.

It is data from the Levada Center that lie behind the bulk of this chapter's analysis of what Russians think. The Levada Center continues to operate independently and to publish survey results as it finds them, and not necessarily as the authorities would like to find them. These findings nonetheless include very high approval rates for President Putin and strongly conservative social attitudes among the Russian people as a whole. The Levada Center's status as an independent public opinion polling agency gained an ironic boost in the eyes of many observers when, in September 2016, it was added to the Russian Ministry of Justice's list of 'foreign agents' on the grounds that it had taken some money from sources in the West and is engaged in what Russia's government interprets as political activity (for more detail on the law requiring named organisations to be formally identified as 'foreign agents', see Chapter Four). For now, the Levada opinion polling agency continues to function as a reliable and absorbing source of insights into what Russians think.

Perhaps appropriately for a chapter on public opinion polling, we have begun by interrogating two questions: what do Russians think? And, can we know what Russians think? As this volume's purpose is to get inside Russian politics, a third question remains significant before exploring Russian public opinion in more depth: namely, does it matter what Russians think? Not 'does it matter?' in a general sense, as of course the opinions of the citizens of the world's largest country matter, but 'does it matter?' in terms of the practice of politics in Russia. Despite its constitutional and institutional framework being democratic, Russia is not a fully functioning democracy for all the various reasons set out in earlier chapters that can be summed up in one bald statement: that those in power in Russia ensure, by a variety of means, that they never lose elections. But public opinion still matters politically. The ruling regime does not dismiss out of hand what people think. On the contrary, it goes out of its way to influence and shape the views of Russia's citizens.

From the perspective of the political scientist attempting to categorise the nature of Russia's political system, it fits well into the type 'disguised dictatorship' that is the go-to mode of authoritarianism in the twenty-first century. The scholar of authoritarianism Paul Brooker talks of a periodisation of authoritarian regime types, beginning with military rule and moving on through one-party states to contemporary disguised dictatorships. In other words, the world has moved on from blatant justifications for authoritarian rule based around naked power or anti-democratic ideologies, so that even authoritarian regimes these days mostly claim adherence to democracy. While for some such states fraudulent and flimsy claims to operating a genuine multi-party democratic system represent little more than a vain veneer, an effective democratic disguise for authoritarianism has to be more convincing.

In essence, the best 'disguised dictatorships' look as much like democracies as possible, while ensuring that the ruling regime maintains its power. Blatant electoral fraud and 95+ per cent majorities – although both are occasionally known in Putin's Russia – serve to undermine the disguise by drawing attention to it. It is much better in this form of authoritarian rule for people to genuinely support the regime. Achieving such an outcome is a two-way street. Yes, the Russian authorities do not flinch from using, among other tools (as set out in Chapter Four), control and influence of the media in order to shape public opinion; but nor are they entirely unmoved by the opinion of Russia's people. As we shall see, anger at élite-level corruption is rife among Russians, and so the regime has embarked on anti-corruption campaigns and the occasional high-profile arrest. Whether such a move marks a genuine effort to combat corruption or a mere sop to mitigate popular anger remains a moot point, but the public mood has some influence. Similarly, presidential election campaigns in Russia involve the shoe-in winner crossing the country, distributing beneficence and boosting public support. He would scarcely bother if such support were of no importance. For the Russian political system to function as it does, public opinion is by no means all; but it still matters.

WHAT BOTHERS RUSSIANS?

Income differentials in Russia are not particularly remarkable at the aggregate level. According to United Nations data, comparing the incomes of the top and bottom 10 per cent reveals Russia to be more egalitarian than the United States and the United Kingdom, but less egalitarian than most West European countries. But income differentials are not the same as wealth differentials. A number of corruption-related causes célèbres stem from the discrepancy between the declared income and the ostentatious expenditure of officials, with newspapers reporting such cases as presidential spokesman Dmitry Peskov sporting a watch worth around £400,000 at his wedding. In 2016, Russian anti-corruption campaigners ran a bus tour around London and stopping at a series of grand properties said to be owned by members of the Putin regime or their associates, including two apartments reportedly worth £10 million that they claimed were owned by Russian Deputy Prime Minister Igor Shuvalov and his wife, despite them costing 100 times Shuvalov's annual salary. As Chapter Three sets out, Russia represents the world's most egregious case in terms of wealth concentration, with Credit Suisse's annual wealth report for 2016 asserting that 75 per cent of the country's wealth is owned by just 1 per cent of the population. The ostentatious wealth of Russia's richest comes up against two particular issues in the court of Russian public opinion. The first surrounds Russian attitudes to inequality. A somewhat hackneyed joke often told by Western observers of Russian society concerns a Russian peasant whose neighbour acquires a new cow. In despair at his own poverty, the poor peasant cries out to God, bemoaning his lot. To his surprise, God answers his cry and asks the peasant what he wants to happen. 'Please Lord,' responds the peasant, 'kill that cow.'

The joke portrays Russians as the sort of people who would prefer that everybody have nothing, rather than a few people have more than everybody else. It was often told by Western entrepreneurs in a slightly superior way in the 1990s as if it were the absence of an entrepreneurial spirit that lay behind Russia's economic difficulties. That said, although there is no ingrained ethnic trait to back up such stereotyping, the joke's origins lie in politics and a Cold War-era comparison of attitudes to property under Communism and capitalism. In an age where popular disquiet over income inequality shapes politics in states throughout the world, it ought not to surprise us if this is particularly the case in Russia, with the residual effect of decades of Soviet egalitarian practice and propaganda being followed by a post-Soviet era in which standards of living plummeted for most, while a few became eye-wateringly rich, acquiring multiple and vast properties, entering the global super-rich 'whose yacht is biggest' competition and buying up football clubs. 'Lord, please kill that cow' doesn't begin to cover it. But, of course, deep disquiet over income inequality is by no means uniquely held by Russians, nor is an attitude that says better for all to share less wealth more equally than for a few to have vastly more in a richer country.

Surveys of Russia's population today show that almost 90 per cent disapprove of sizeable differences in wealth. Similarly, the British Social Attitudes Survey reported in 2012 that 82 per cent of Britons considered the income gap in the UK to be too large, and a YouGov survey in 2014 informed us that, in Britain, '56% would like to see a more equal distribution, even if it reduces the total amount of wealth'. When pollsters from the Levada Center ask Russians about tensions in society, more than three quarters say that there are strong or very strong tensions between the rich and the poor; a far higher proportion of people than those who see similar tensions between people of different nationalities (52 per cent), followers of different religions (48 per cent) or between the young and the old (27 per cent).

The second issue particularly likely to colour Russian attitudes to the wealthy relates to the manner in which many of the super-rich have acquired their money. The perception is widely held that Russia's business and political élite, many of whom overlap, are mired in corruption. When Russians were asked in 2016 to identify the biggest obstacle on the path to their country's development, the top three issues named were the corruption of the authorities (49 per cent), the authorities thinking only of themselves and ignoring the interests of society (27 per cent), and the failure of officials to implement the laws and decrees that are in place (26 per cent). In essence, these three obstacles on the road to Russia's future development amount to different aspects of the same problem. Furthermore, such a negative view of the authorities and officials as that held by Russians today does not relate only to the Russia of Vladimir Putin, since an identical survey carried out in 1998 came up with virtually the same results during the presidency of Boris Yeltsin.

We can assert with some confidence, then, that frustration about corrupt officialdom represents a widespread feeling among Russians, who see corruption as a major barrier facing their country's development. What is more, this common perception of affairs goes back at least a couple of decades. Again, Russians' attitudes and perceptions are not particularly unusual. We noted above the similarities between Russian and British views on the undesirability of a large income gap in society. Similarly, a major EU-wide survey carried out by Eurobarometer in 2014 showed that more than one in three EU citizens thought corruption to be a major problem, with 43 per cent of people in the EU's fifteen 'new member states' perceiving corruption to be 'very widespread'. Questions around the magnitude of corrupt activity are significant. For our purpose here, though, they are worthy of note also because they demonstrate what perhaps should not – but too often does – need demonstrating: the normality of Russians and their opinions. People are people the world over, particularly when it comes to generalisable attitudes and opinions at the national level. Of course, specific circumstances influence attitudes and culture. The national story cannot but help impact public opinion, and Russians are by no means immune to such an impact. For the most part, however, the Russian people are bothered about what bothers people anywhere: standards of living, the well-being of their families and security.

WHAT RUSSIANS REALLY THINK OF THEIR LEADERS

For the interested but casual observer in the West, it would be fairly easy to gain the impression that the people of Russia represent an oppressed population, desperate but unable to throw off the yoke of an authoritarian ruling regime. While the epithet 'authoritarian' fits – though with a range of comparative caveats about degrees and definitions – the Russian people as a whole are not a boiling cauldron about to blow their top. At least not so far as having a desperate desire for Western-style democracy or to overthrow Vladimir Putin goes. President Putin has an approval rating that would be the envy of politicians anywhere, sitting as it does between 60 per cent and 80 per cent for the vast majority of his time as President. The lowest ratings came on his return to the presidency for a third term in 2012 when, as economic performance struggled, his performance in the role of President was approved of by a 'mere' 60 per cent of Russians. What, by Putin's standards, was a low rating rocketed upwards beyond 80 per cent in the first few months of 2014, coincidental with the ramping up of patriotic fervour that accompanied the Winter Olympics in Sochi and, more significantly, the annexation of Crimea.

Are these high ratings for President Putin genuine? In the sense that they are the results of scientifically rigorous surveys carried out by independent and trained pollsters, then yes, these high levels of approval are genuine. Critics dismiss them, however, not on the grounds that they may have been crudely forged, but that there are other factors at play that massage public opinion data in favour of the President. Specifically, two criticisms come to the fore: first, that media coverage of Vladimir Putin is so relentlessly positive that it is small wonder that most Russians approve of his deeds; second, and more ominously, that respondents to opinion polls on the question of whether they approve of the ruling regime or not are disinclined to give an honest answer for fear – however unfounded – that it will somehow count against them. It is difficult to give a precise measurement of the influence, or not, of these factors.

First, with regard to the impact of media coverage, certainly, mass media coverage of Vladimir Putin in Russia does not go out of its way to present the people with much reason to be critical, though even here observers would do well to credit the Russian people with the intelligence, education and appropriate degree of scepticism that they possess. Consider, for example, Putin's almost annual publicity stunts. These have gained global notoriety, with the figure of a bare-chested Russian President on horseback becoming an instant identifier for satirists across the Western world. Other stunts have included shooting a tiger (though, in the spirit of 21st-century image-making, with a tranquilliser dart rather than a bullet), leading a flock of migrating cranes over Siberia in a motorised hang glider, working out in a gym with Prime Minister Dmitry Medvedev and finding two ancient Greek urns while scuba diving in the Black Sea. Russians are as capable as anyone of seeing such exploits for the gimmicky and carefully scripted attention grabbers that they are. After all, there can be no sense of superior sniffiness in a Western political culture that saw the President of the United States trek across the Alaskan wilderness with British TV's 'survival expert' Bear Grylls. When it comes to action man PR, Vladimir Putin may be the trend-setter, but others have followed. Why then, when Putin engages in such activities, is reaction in the Western media so scornful? Why does the serious-minded *Economist* magazine call 'these preposterous photo ops … part of the increasingly sinister personality cult the Kremlin has cultivated around Mr Putin'?

The answer is multifaceted, even after taking the negativity of *The Economist* towards Putin for granted. An awareness of the lack of democratic choice in Russia might partly explain such disdain; after all, in democracies leaders reluctantly submit themselves to these activities in order to gain votes, so, the thinking goes, why does the President of an authoritarian regime like Russia feel the need to behave in this way? Such an explanation, however, can only be partial. Even with its democratic deficit, the Russian system still has elections and the Putin regime still courts popularity (and in any case, Barack Obama's Alaskan trek came towards the end of his second term and so served no electoral purpose). An element of the scorn directed at President Putin's bare-chested posturing stems also from cultural differences. Much Western media, although happy to report the photo opportunities of their countries' leaders, tend towards greater scepticism than the Russian media when doing so. When a scuba-diving Vladimir Putin emerged from beneath the surf clutching relics from ancient Greece, Russia's international news channel RT reported without apparent irony – or with such subtle irony that it was undetectable by RT's Western readers and viewers – that 'to everyone's utter surprise, he managed to find two ancient amphorae dating back to the sixth century AD'. RT's enthusiastic reporting was itself undercut some weeks later when Putin's spokesman Dmitry Peskov candidly admitted what everyone knew to be the case anyway – that the urns had been placed on the seabed in advance and Putin instructed as to their whereabouts.

The point of this diversion into Putin's photo opportunities is to undermine the notion that Russians gullibly lap up such fripperies any more than you or I would. Spending time on Russian social media would very soon provide sufficient reassurance that it is not from publicity stunts and propagandising that the popularity of Vladimir Putin stems. The Russian population is well versed in spotting propagandistic cant; after all, many of them have experience of the Soviet era.

What, then, about the idea that Russians do not tell opinion pollsters their true feelings concerning the President for fear that it is either not the 'done' thing, or that to do so would bring some form of retribution against them? As well as asking respondents whether they approve of Vladimir Putin's actions as President, the Levada polling agency also regularly asks a whole series of detailed questions about Vladimir Putin and his relationship with the Russian people. Most pertinent to our discussion here, Levada's pollsters examine whether people feel able to respond openly to questions relating to the authorities and to President Putin in particular. Almost half of respondents consider that Russians deem themselves able to respond openly to such questions; one third think that only around half of the population feel able to answer openly; and only 17 per cent believe that most people sense a need to hide their true feelings in this respect.

In early 2017, four American political scientists published a detailed, peer-reviewed article assessing, through a series of list experiments, claims that the Russian population dissembles to pollsters when asked for their thoughts on Putin.[*]

---

[*] Timothy Frye, Scott Gehlbach, Kyle L. Marquardt & Ora John Reuter (2017), 'Is Putin's popularity real?', *Post-Soviet Affairs*, 33:1, 1–15, DOI: 10.1080/1060586X.2016.1144334, http://dx.doi.org/10.1080/1060586X.2016.1144334

They found – in surveys undertaken during 2015 – an 80 per cent approval rating for the President and little evidence of dishonest respondents. Their conclusion was that Putin's approval ratings largely reflect the attitudes of the Russian population, and that, if anything, they may even understate Russians' support for their President.

Positive attitudes towards Putin stem from his longevity in the position of head of state – or, at least, 'national leader', considering that he was Prime Minister between 2008 and 2012 – as well as from admiration towards his achievements and him as a leader. One can generalise about Russians' attitudes towards their leaders with regard to a tradition of venerating – though not in every case – the man at the top, at the same time as holding a deep scepticism towards the authorities in general. In the pre-revolutionary years, the Tsar was known as the 'little father', second only to Father God in overseeing the welfare of his people; Communist dictator Josef Stalin (1928–1953) benefited from a cult built around his self-proclaimed position as the 'Great Leader'; and Vladimir Putin has achieved a certain standing as Russia's national leader that seems to protect him to *some* extent from the natural criticism and blame that a people directs towards its government.

The extent to which Putin's status depends on his achievements, as opposed to his reputation and pre-eminent position, is illuminated by a series of more specific questions posed by the Levada Center. When asked in 2016 who should receive the credit for economic successes and the rise in living standards of the Russian people, 56 per cent said Vladimir Putin, 20 per cent said the Russian government and 12 per cent said current Prime Minister and former President Dmitry Medvedev. At the same time, when asked who should take the blame for problems in the country and the increase in the cost of living, 50 per cent said the government, 32 per cent said Dmitry Medvedev and 40 per cent said Vladimir Putin. From the institutional and empirical perspective, there is no obvious reason why the President should gain credit for economic success but not blame for economic failure. There is something deeper going on in the veneration of Vladimir Putin.

Levada's more detailed questions about attitudes towards Putin are helpful when it comes to digging a little below the simplistic headlines about approval. The agency asked in 2016 what words best express people's attitude towards Vladimir Putin. A third of respondents said that they could not say anything bad about him, while the most popular single word that expresses how Russians feel about their President was, interestingly, 'sympathy'. This seems a surprising emotion to sum up what many Russians feel when they think of their President, speaking as it does of a deeper and more nuanced attitude than we might expect. Not awe, or respect, or even adoration, but sympathy. The attitude here chimes with popular perceptions concerning a sense among Russians, when it comes to leaders of a particular standing, that they are contending on behalf of the people, faced with tremendous challenges and let down by the authorities beneath them.

When asked what impresses them most about President Putin, the top three most impressive aspects, in order, were that he is an experienced politician, he is energetic, decisive and strong-willed and he is far-sighted. If, as the pollsters did, you turn this around and ask people what they don't like about Putin, the most striking feature of responses is that over 50 per cent of Russians declare the question to be too difficult to answer, or else claim that they like everything about him. Nonetheless, of those who did admit to not liking some things about their President, the most disliked features were his ties with big capital and with corrupt politicians (17 per cent each). According to this opinion poll, more than 10 per cent of Russians think that the interests of the people are alien to Putin. Quizzing citizens on those areas where they consider President Putin to have been unsuccessful, the standout issues year after year have been a failure to deal with corruption and to restrain the oligarchs. That corruption is the central front on which Alexei Navalny fights his oppositionist campaigns makes Navalny more of a threat to the regime than those who oppose Putinism on more abstract and less relatable grounds. Of particular note is that, by the end of 2016, more than half of Russians who took part agreed with the assertion that Vladimir Putin is guilty of those abuses of power of which his opponents accuse him. For now, while Putin remains in a strong position of power, Russians appear able to hold such a view alongside remarkably high approval rates for the President. But such an inherent tension remains potentially problematic for the regime should some particular event or revelation result in a decisive shift in popular opinion.

WHAT RUSSIANS THINK OF THE NON-SYSTEMIC OPPOSITION

A good deal of attention is given in the Western media to Russian opposition figures who fight for greater democracy and against the abuses of the ruling regime. Although not without impact in Russia, these members of the 'non-systemic' opposition – that is, opposition beyond the three 'opposition' parties in parliament who for the most part accept and cooperate with the rule of the Putin regime – are far less well-known and enjoy far lower levels of support within Russia as a whole than the amount of coverage that they receive in the West might indicate. When the All-Russia Public Opinion Research Center (VTsIOM) presented its regular 'which politicians do you trust?' poll findings in May 2017, at the bottom of the list came Alexei Navalny, with a score of 1.1 per cent, compared to President Putin's 50.7 per cent trust rating.

Such a finding is not to be dismissed – it is to be interrogated and interpreted. We have already noted that the All-Russia Public Opinion Research Center came under so much state pressure that its founders moved on in protest to establish the independent Levada Center polling agency during the early years of the Putin regime. It is not wholly independent of state influence. Furthermore, any assessment of opinion polls must always consider the question asked, as opposed to the way the results are reported. In the case of the All-Russia Public Opinion Research Center's survey, the findings are reported under the heading 'Trust in Politicians', but respondents were not given a list of politicians and asked whom they trust. They were specifically asked to come up for themselves with the names of political figures to be trusted 'with important matters of state'; no names were presented from which they might select. There is evidently some question bias present; after all, since the century began 'important matters of state' have been in the hands of either Vladimir Putin or Dmitry Medvedev (who had fallen from second to fourth in the 'most trusted' list by mid-May 2017, with a meagre 14.9 per cent, during a period in which Navalny's allegations of corruption continued to haunt him). The question is also implicitly testing the knowledge of respondents with regard to political actors in Russia, and Russians are no more likely to follow politics closely than do the general population in other European countries. If people have scarcely heard of Alexei Navalny, they are unlikely to proffer his name without prompting. All that said, it is not unbelievable that only around 1 per cent of Russians would think to suggest Navalny's name when asked whom they might trust with important matters of state.

The more independent Levada polling agency, aware that the mass media in Russia are sparing in their coverage of opposition politicians, asks more astute questions than those posed by the All-Russia Public Opinion Research Center. Their polls regularly question the extent to which Russians are aware of the leaders and the activities of opposition movements. Ahead of the parliamentary elections in December 2016, Levada carried out a poll asking people whether they had heard of – note, not whether they supported – the Democratic Coalition that had been established by a group of leading figures and parties from the non-systemic opposition. Almost 60 per cent of respondents replied that being asked the question was the first time they had ever heard of this coalition. Only 13 per cent of those asked were confident that they had heard of it. What is going on here is not some sort of blanket ban on the coverage of opposition politicians by the state media. After all, Alexei Navalny did come second in the Moscow mayoral election of 2013, and opposition figures took part in debates and political discussion programmes on national television as usual ahead of the 2016 parliamentary election. Those who are interested enough to find out about and follow the opposition can do so via social media, interviews in certain sections of the press and broadcast media and so on, but for opposition figures to break through to the mainstream, more is needed. Indeed, not all Russians are part of the internet generation or interested in politics. What is more, the lack of detailed coverage can tend to lump opponents of the regime together, as if they are all of one mind. Such an approach plays into the regime's narrative that those who oppose it are somehow lackeys of the West – fifth columnists who are traitors to Russia.

Even the Levada polling agency has played into such a perception. A poll in 2015 asked respondents whether they were sympathetic to the non-systemic opposition, 'such people as

Mikhail Kasyanov, Alexei Navalny, Boris Nemtsov, Vladimir Ryzhkov and others'. That's OK up to a point, since these figures can be bracketed together as non-systemic opponents of the Putin regime. But to present them as though they are identical in their views provides a problematic question and response. The veterans of the non-systemic opposition are more likely to focus on arguments about democratic process and rights, as well as to be fairly frequent travellers to the West. Such a position has comparatively little support in Russia. Given a choice between three potential political systems – the Soviet, contemporary Russian and Western democracy – by far the least popular choice among respondents to Levada pollsters in 2016 was the latter, supported by a mere 13 per cent. Opinion polls regularly show that about two thirds of Russians consider the breakup of the Soviet Union in a negative light. Unlike many in the non-systemic opposition, Navalny focuses less on abstract ideas about government, but rather on corruption among the ruling élite. He has also garnered some reputation for holding relatively nationalist views. To be identified to some degree with Russian nationalism is to be far closer to the mainstream of Russian public opinion than to be identified with Western-style liberal democracy.

RUSSIANS, NATIONALISM AND CONSERVATISM

It is a commonplace to say that people are generally far more bothered about their individual and family economic circumstances than they are about more abstract concepts such as democracy or the standing of the nation. While that generalisation has been true in Russia for most of this century, opinion polls show that Russians became particularly engaged with questions of international status and military standing after the annexation of Crimea in 2014, and the accompanying domestic propaganda that seemed to put Russia almost on a war footing. In the decade preceding that annexation, the Levada Center's poll ratings of the achievements of Vladimir Putin consistently had economic development and living standards at the head of the list. The standard policy areas were usurped in 2014 by 'strengthening Russia's international position'. In the 2016 version of these ratings, top of the poll came the heightening of Russia's military preparedness, with 14 per cent selecting this as Putin's key achievement, when it had bumped along at 1 or 2 per cent throughout most of the century's opening decade.

In a Levada survey in 2016, 77 per cent of Russians answered yes to the question 'do you consider yourself to be a Russian patriot?'. This figure was unchanged from 2000. A Gallup poll in the United States in 2016 reported that 81 per cent of US citizens were either 'extremely' (52 per cent) or 'very' (29 per cent) proud to be an American. Britons tend to wear their national pride more quietly, with a British social attitudes survey from 2013 reporting that, although 82 per cent of respondents overall described themselves as proud to be British, only 35 per cent went for the 'very proud' option. Comparatively speaking then, Russians are about as patriotic – actually a little less – as Americans and Britons. As Chapter

Seven sets out in detail, however, patriotic and nationalist feeling in Russia tends to be tied in with attitudes concerning Russia's position in the world with regard to the West. Understandably, Russians' attitudes towards the West when it comes to simplistic favourable/unfavourable survey questions vary according to the state of international relations. According to the Pew Research Center, favourable attitudes among Russians towards the United States plummeted from 41 per cent to 15 per cent between 2007 and 2015, and towards the EU from 62 to 31 per cent over the same period. More stable is the perception that is held by many Russians of what the West denotes; specifically, that it represents 'another civilisation, a different world' – a view reported to Levada pollsters by 48 per cent of respondents in 2008 and 44 per cent in 2016.

Official Russian discourse, particularly since the conservative turn marked by Vladimir Putin's return to the presidency in 2012, has talked in civilisational terms of Russia standing up for the traditional values that Europe in particular, and the West more widely, has abandoned. When it comes to attitudes towards sexuality and relationships, Russians differ markedly from their contemporary Western counterparts. According to a report published by the Pew Research Center in May 2017, 85 per cent of Russians view homosexuality as morally wrong and say that it should not be accepted by society. Levels of support for same-sex marriage in Russia are notably low, at around 5 per cent. Such social attitudes are difficult to interrogate on their own, since they have become part of the 'culture war' raging between Russia and the West in recent years. The word 'gayropa' – a neologism from 'gay' and 'Europa' – has gained wide recognition in Russia as a signifier of a dissolute Europe that has jettisoned long-accepted standards of sexual morality. In his annual address to parliament in 2013, President Putin criticised those 'many nations' that are changing ethical norms in what he called 'this destruction of traditional values from above ... contrary to the will of the majority'. In turn, Russian policy with regard to homosexuality has been widely criticised by Western interlocutors. The concept of 'gayropa' has come to mark a geo-cultural border that has made discussion of policy and legislation around homosexuality difficult to consider as a subject separate from the wider complex of declining East–West relations.

Whether Russian social attitudes with regard to sexuality and gay rights would change were there to be an improvement in international relations remains a matter of conjecture. It is similarly speculative to suggest that attitudes will shift in this regard as generational change inevitably occurs. If, as usually happens, spatial comparisons are made between Russia and the Orthodox world on the one hand, and the rest of Europe on the other, then the differing attitudes with regard to sexuality are stark. If, however, temporal comparisons are made within the spatial, then differences diminish to some extent. Looking back a few decades, British Social Attitudes Survey data from 1987 reported that 75 per cent of the UK population believed homosexuality to be wrong; 64 per cent thought it 'always wrong', while 11 per cent went for 'mostly wrong'. More than thirty years later, attitudes in Britain have been transformed. Such an attitudinal transformation *could* occur in Russia. The fact that there is little evidence pointing in that direction at the moment – 84 per cent of young Russian adults (eighteen to thirty-four) consider that homosexuality should not be accepted by society, compared to 88 per cent of Russians over thirty-four – does not in itself rule out such a transformation, though it does make plain the scale of any such shift in social attitudes that would be required for that transformation to occur.

If differing attitudes on homosexuality provide a marker of a large gap between Russian and Western values, the same cannot be said of another policy area that is very much to the fore in contemporary European politics: immigration. Comparing Russian and British data reveals that the people of the Russian Federation and the United Kingdom are, to a large extent, of one mind on the subject of immigrants, and that the marginal differences that can be found actually indicate a slightly less liberal line among Britons than among Russians. In 2013, the British Social Attitudes Survey published a report on what people in the UK think of immigration. On the basic question of levels of immigration – although the question does not match precisely with that asked by the Levada Center and used in our comparison here – 77 per cent of Britons wanted immigration to be reduced by either a lot (56 per cent) or a little (21 per cent). Similarly, when Russians were asked in 2013 how they respond to the popular right-wing slogan 'Russia for the Russians', 66 per cent of them supported it, of whom 23 per cent saw the implementation of this goal as a matter of urgency, and 43 per cent wanted it implemented 'but within sensible limits'.

Singling out two of the key aspects in debates around immigration – its economic and cultural effects – again reveals strong similarities in the views of Russians and Britons. In the UK in 2013, 47 per cent considered the economic impact of immigration to be negative; in Russia in 2012 (figures for 2013 are not available), 43 per cent thought that on the whole immigrants did not contribute to the development of the Russian economy. When it comes to culture, again comparing the United Kingdom in 2013 with Russia in 2012, 45 per cent of Britons thought that immigration undermined British culture, whereas 39 per cent of Russians considered that on the whole immigrants erode Russian culture. Comparing these data, not only are the similarities in attitude apparent, but in all of the comparisons it is British attitudes to immigration that are, in fact, marginally less liberal than Russian attitudes.

CHAPTER SEVEN

RUSSIAN CIVILISATION

CULTURE IN THE MOSCOW STATE CONSERVATORY

In central Moscow, a ten minute stroll from the Kremlin, a bronze statue of the great composer Pyotr Tchaikovsky sits mounted on a red granite pedestal in front of the Moscow State Conservatory. The Conservatory is one of the centres of Russian culture. An internationally renowned institution, it is the alma mater of scores of musical greats, including Soviet giants such as the pianist Sviatoslav Richter, the violinist David Oistrakh and the cellist Mstislav Rostropovich. The conductor Gennadi Rozhdestvensky, a former chief conductor of the BBC Symphony Orchestra who was presented with an honorary CBE by the Princess Royal in 2014, was taught conducting at the Conservatory under the tutelage of his father, the great Soviet conductor Nikolai Anosov. Eminent figures of international repute in contemporary classical music, including the pianist Boris Berezovsky and the violinist Viktoria Mullova, graduated from the Conservatory, too.

In March 2017, however, the Moscow State Conservatory hit the headlines for reasons far removed from its musical excellence when it became the latest and most illustrious educational institution to feature in a series of online exposés of political proselytisation by staff in Russian classrooms. A student at this élite establishment uploaded a video of a seminar in which a fellow composition student was instructed by the lecturer to read out to the rest of the class a document detailing the deeds of alleged traitors and fifth columnists in contemporary Russia. The crassness of such a pedagogical – or rather, propagandist – technique unsurprisingly failed to impress students of the calibre necessary to enter the Moscow State Conservatory. They took the opportunity, as self-respecting students the world over ought, to ridicule so obtuse an exercise. Those named as traitors were not even violent usurpers of public order or convicted criminals, but included relatively mainstream if predominantly liberal public figures with national profiles. The lecturer herself, seemingly unprepared for such a derisive reaction, is said to have responded to the students' apparent disdain for the process with threats to hinder further study at the Conservatory.

What were students at an internationally renowned music college doing in a class of this nature? Why were Russia's finest young musicians required to participate in the denunciation of those who oppose the Putin regime? Moscow media soon reported that the academic leading the class was a relatively new member of staff who had been employed by the Conservatory to teach a course called 'The Basics of the Cultural

Politics of Russia' that had been recommended for the curriculum by the Ministry of Culture. Whether the incident has had any long-lasting negative impact on the recalcitrant students' progress remains unclear, but it may have influenced the career of the lecturer. Students and staff of the Conservatory reportedly petitioned its Rector for the resignation of the academic leading the course, and within days she had gone.

Nor was this the only incident of its type. It came amidst a wave of similar online revelations, albeit that most of them were recordings from provincial schools rather than élite higher education institutions in Moscow. The pattern repeated itself, as teachers instructed, and sometimes berated, students about the dangers posed to Russia by Western liberalism and popular anti-corruption demonstrations. In the days immediately preceding the anti-corruption demonstrations of March 2017, reports of teachers discouraging their students from participating in these were posted on social media from cities across Russia – Bryansk, Komsomolsk-on-Amur, Krasnoyarsk, Orenburg, Tomsk, Rostov-on-Don and Vladimir. In June 2017, a secondary school teacher in Krasnodar region told the local news site that he had been sacked from his job for attending an anti-corruption rally, after a court sentenced him to ten days in prison for violating Russia's law on public meetings.

TEACHING RUSSIAN VALUES

The politicisation of curriculum content in support of Russia's ruling regime contains echoes of two particular occurrences in Russia's history over the last century or so. The first is the rise of the student protest movement in the 1890s and beyond. The sight of hundreds of angry students being attacked by the police as they took to the streets of St Petersburg and Moscow to demonstrate against the policies of a reactionary conservative government became commonplace in those pre-revolutionary years. Beginning with specific complaints about university life, these demonstrations took on regime-changing intensity as the students increasingly engaged in common purpose with wider social forces, culminating in the socio-political breakdown of the 1905 revolution. As Chapter Four sets out, student engagement with the anti-corruption demonstrations of 2017 has had its own impact. For the purposes of this chapter, however, political influence in the classroom has echoes of more recent, Soviet-era practices.

To indulge in a little personal reminiscence, the knowledge that students at the Moscow State Conservatory were compelled to take a course on 'The Basics of the Cultural Politics of Russia' recommended by the Ministry of Culture put me in mind of my own student days in the 1980s, some of which were spent in the Soviet Union at Voronezh State University in southern-European Russia. With accommodation consisting of four students per each cramped room, it was easy to become acquainted with the studying habits of one's peers. During exam season the mood was generally serious and studious, except for one evening when my roommates' approach to revision seemed positively light-hearted and dismissive. Looking for an explanation, I asked 'What's tomorrow's exam?' 'Marxism–Leninism', came the reply. Students in Soviet universities, and those of the Soviet bloc in Eastern Europe, had to take courses on Communist ideology throughout their studies. The content was ordained by the state and took the form of propaganda rather than critical discussion. For most students, the classes were at best a necessary inconvenience, soporific in nature and didactic in content.

As with many resonances of the Soviet era in today's Russia, compulsory classes in 'The Basics of the Cultural Politics of Russia' remain for now a mere shadow of their Soviet-era precursor. As well as being totally different in curriculum content, they also lack the longevity and ubiquity of the unified 'Basics of Marxism–Leninism' course introduced across Soviet universities at the height of the Stalinist terror in 1938. What is more, we live in a different world now from a time when state capacity was all but sufficient to control the flow of information. Contemporary Russia takes its place in a globalised world where information technology is commonplace and any bored schoolchild or angry student can publish their lessons online in minutes. Knowledge of the world beyond Russia's borders and familiarity with a diverse range of views undermine the efficacy of old-style propaganda. If the state is to succeed in indoctrinating Russia's students – a highly doubtful proposition – then it requires a more sophisticated approach than that essayed at the Moscow State Conservatory.

For all that might undermine the effectiveness of state attempts to propagate the political views of Russia's ruling regime in classrooms and lecture theatres, however, the fact remains that such attempts are still being made. They would have been unthinkable in the immediate post-Soviet years, when Russia's new – and still extant – constitution boldly broke with the authoritarian past and declared that no longer would Russia have an official ideology. Similarly, in the early years of the Putin regime, attempts backed by the Russian Orthodox Church to introduce compulsory classes on 'The Fundamentals of Orthodox Culture' across Russia were undermined as the Ministry of Education supported instead voluntary classes, with pupils choosing between courses on individual faiths, world religion or secular ethics. Such openness and plurality was the norm in many spheres, as it seemed that the idea of one-sided propaganda, painting those who disagree as enemies of the state and cuckolds of the West, had had its day. Not only did it not sit well with Russia's self-proclaimed commitment to being a European nation and its good relations with many Western states, but it would not work anymore.

In the second decade of this century, the Russian state has started to become a little more prescriptive and traditional in its approach to teaching young Russians. As noted above, the line taken in today's Russia is not – and could not be – as trenchant and ubiquitous as that taken by the Soviet state. The Soviet Union, like the other European dictatorships of the twentieth century, existed during what, for would-be totalitarian regimes, was the technological sweet spot. Communication technology was sufficiently developed to enable widespread indoctrination and surveillance on the part of the state, at the same time as the limitations of that technology facilitated state control of the desired geographical and ideological borders. It is much harder to do that with today's information technology, which is not to assert that Russia's ruling regime would want to tread such a path were it even possible. Nonetheless, what we have seen, particularly since the decisive break of Crimea's annexation in 2014, represents a more emboldened and concerted effort to inculcate in Russia's educational institutions, and indeed in society more widely, the values and attitudes that its rulers believe to be desirable. These are not new in themselves, as an emphasis on national unity and the traditional conservative tenets of 'the Russian idea' has been present in official discourse since at least the mid-1990s. There is no doubt, however, that a more emphatic supportive framework has now been constructed to aid the task.

CULTURE AND CIVILISATION

When the term 'culture' is employed in Russian political discourse, it covers a wider range than merely art, literature and so on. To take a class on 'The Basics of the Cultural Politics of Russia' is to be taught about a wider construct; about Russian civilisation. The category 'civilisation' reasserted itself in discussion of international politics after Communism's utopian vision all but disappeared at the end of the 1980s. With the

Soviet Union gone, few people – and almost no state – continued to believe that the Communist alternative represented humanity's future. Even nascent Communist superpower China moved rapidly away from Marx's conceptualisation as any reliable indicator of direction of travel, diluting its nominal adherence to the ideology with generous measures of Western capitalism and ancient Chinese Confucianism. Analysts and thinkers, bereft of the Marxist metanarrative that had served as a catalyst for political and economic debate throughout most of the twentieth century, looked elsewhere for interpretive and predictive frameworks.

In the academic world, two American scholars put forward differing ideas of what the collapse of Communism meant in global terms. For Francis Fukuyama it ushered in 'the end of history', as over time liberal democracy would become the preferred destination of states across the world. Samuel Huntington, on the other hand, foresaw a 'clash of civilisations', in which the bifurcated ideological differences of the Cold War would give way to a complex of international conflict based on something deeper and more elemental than ideological disagreement. That 'something' would spring from the cultural DNA of differing people groups, as conflicting norms, traditions and worldviews led to clashes in an increasingly interconnected and globalised world. US President George Bush Sr's initial post-Soviet optimism about a 'new world order' of international cooperation appeared – with a savage irony that would take another quarter of a century to become apparent – to have got off to a 'good' start in the short and successful first Gulf War against Saddam Hussein's Iraq in 1990–1991. This internationalist hiatus, however, turned out to be more desert mirage than 'Desert Storm' (the epithet given to the US-led military operation against Saddam's forces in 2003). The rising force in the 1990s was not internationalism but nationalism and, to coin a term, 'civilisationalism'.

This chapter began by reporting events at the Moscow State Conservatory, when a clumsily delivered course on 'The Basics of the Cultural Politics of Russia' backfired badly. But where does such a course even come from, and why was it being taught in an élite institution of musical education? Its immediate origins go back to December 2014, the end of a year that had seen a dramatic ramping up of Russian national-patriotism on the back of military action in Ukraine and a decisive culmination of years of increasingly assertive anti-Westernism. It is scarcely an exaggeration to say that, in Russia, public opinion was put on a war footing. On 24 December, a presidential decree was issued 'On the Basics of State Cultural Policy'. Cultural policy sounds harmless enough if it concerns, as sections of this presidential decree do, 'literature, music, opera, ballet, theatre, film' and so on and their place in the national economy. But the meaning of 'culture' in Russian state policy is not so straightforward.

The 2014 decree talks of how the state's cultural policy forms an essential part of the Russian Federation's national security policy, and of how cultural policy underlies 'state sovereignty and the civilisational identity of the country'.

What we are dealing with here is not simply art as culture, but a fundamentally Huntingtonian understanding of what culture is. Samuel Huntington's famous 'clash of civilisations' thesis, as noted above, saw international conflict after the Cold War arising out of cultural differences between various multitudinous groupings that he identified within the world's population – Islamic, Sinic, African, Hindu, Japanese, Latin American, Western and Orthodox. When the Russian state talks about cultural policy and its significance for national security, state sovereignty and civilisational identity, it has in mind the whole complex of attitudes, beliefs and history that make Russia Russia and Russians, well, Russians. It embraces the notion that this is more than nationalism: it is civilisationalism. When students in the Moscow State Conservatory are taught about the basics of state cultural policy, it's not Tchaikovsky that they're studying; it's how to be a proper Russian. Or, to use the wording of the decree itself, it is:

the strengthening of civil identity, the creation of conditions for bringing up citizens, the preservation of historical and cultural traits and the use of these in upbringing and education, the transfer from one generation to the next of those values that are traditional in Russian civilisation – our norms, traditions, customs and ways of behaving.

It would be simplistic to depict Russia on this point as out of step with democratic practice, decrying the reintroduction of Soviet-style indoctrination in the education system at the behest of an authoritarian state. Comparing Russian sensitivities about the loss of national identity among the younger generation in the globalising world of the twenty-first century to a similar mood in other European countries might prompt a less judgemental interpretation. After all, in 2014 the Ministry of Education of the United Kingdom brought in a change of regulations to require the embedding of 'British values' in schools, in order to tighten up standards with regard to the spiritual, moral, social and cultural development of pupils. In the UK, those values are democracy, the rule of law, individual liberty and mutual respect for and tolerance of those with different – and no – faiths and beliefs. In comparison, the Russian list of values both differs from and overlaps with the British list, as well as adding many more aspects with a more programmatic conservative and statist tone. The Russian state developed a whole series of documents from 2014 onwards dealing with the subject of national culture and patriotic education. In none of these did the word democracy appear, and only a passing nod was made to the rule of law – notable omissions given that Article 1 of the Russian Constitution straightforwardly proclaims that 'Russia is a democratic federal law-governed state'. The concepts of individual liberty and mutual tolerance, on the other hand, received plentiful reinforcement.

In 2015 Russia's government published two documents: a 'Strategy for the Development of Education in the Russian Federation in the Period up to 2025' and a 'State Programme for the Patriotic Education of Citizens of the Russian

Federation, 2016–2020'.* Of particular interest for our argument here and alongside a range of laudable aims that would be uncontroversial in most states in the developed world, these documents assert the state's role in educating young patriots. The broad strategy on the development of education in Russia from 2015 to 2025 speaks of creating children who are proud of their homeland and ready to defend its interests. 'Defend' here does not have a purely rhetorical sense, as a programme of military-patriotic education forms part of the strategy. The strategy also promotes educating children in the spiritual values of Russia. These and more are expanded upon in the specific programme for patriotic education, with its boasts of how centres for military-patriotic education and military training of youths have already been established in seventy-eight of Russia's eighty-three regions. As well as training Russia's youth in military matters, the programme also speaks of training up qualified specialists in patriotic education.

It may be that the training of specialists in patriotic education to work with the nation's youth played a part in the surge of reported cases, noted at the beginning of this chapter, of teachers warning their pupils to be wary of those who protest against the state. Despite parallels that can be drawn between aspects of Russian practice and the increase in recent years of patriotic education in democratic countries, within the Russian context there exists a blurring between the upholding

---

* The word translated in these titles as 'education' is *vospitanie* and has strong connotations of upbringing more widely rather than a narrow focus on formal education.

of Russian values in general, and specific support for the ruling regime. Just over a year after the presidential decree on cultural policy, the Russian government issued a 'Strategy on State Cultural Policy to 2030' (February 2016). Its tone reinforces the implication that those who do not agree with the stance of the Putin regime are somehow anti-Russian, from where it is but a small step to the labelling of opponents of the regime as traitors and fifth columnists. According to this strategy, among the most dangerous threats to the future of the Russian Federation are the devaluing of generally accepted values, the negative evaluation of significant periods of Russia's history, the spread of false statements about Russia's historical backwardness, the breaking of family ties and the growth of individualism. On top of these, specific threats to national security in the area of culture include the erosion of traditional Russian spiritual-moral values, the distribution of low quality products of mass culture and the 'propaganda of permissiveness'. There is plenty of scope within that mix of vague insinuations, implicit anti-Westernism and dog-whistle phrasing to label those who oppose the regime as active threats to the future of Russia and its national security.

PROPAGANDISING RUSSIAN CIVILISATION

During the US presidential campaign of 2016, allegations of Russian interference in the election were rife, and particularly so after the American people had voted President Trump into office. While there were plenty of accusations, the availability of hard evidence to back them up was in short supply. As demand increased for more than anger and finger-pointing in the public domain, the Central Intelligence Agency (CIA), the Federal Bureau of Investigation (FBI) and the National Security Agency (NSA) of the United States published a rare joint report a fortnight before the President's inauguration, outlining the unclassified elements of their evidence. Of the thirteen pages of the report proper, six were taken up with a description of the activities of the English language TV channel RT America, part of an international broadcasting network set up and funded by the Russian government. This Intelligence Community Assessment raised some very pertinent questions about whether the activities of a TV channel pushing the line of a foreign state constitutes unusual and unacceptable interference in the elections of another state, even quoting Russia Today (RT) Editor in Chief Margarita Simonyan's tweet that '[US] Ambassador McFaul hints that our channel is interference with US domestic affairs. And we, sinful souls, were thinking that it is freedom of speech'. Leaving aside any judgement on that matter, the evolution of RT illustrates the increasing resources that Russia has put into defending and propagating its view of the world in recent years.

As with other domestic aspects of the promotion of the Putin regime's worldview, the international propagation of news with a regime-friendly angle has become more forceful, and frankly less sophisticated in terms of content, over recent years. The international TV news channel Russia

Today – funded by the Russian government, with a staff of around 2,000 and broadcasting in English, Spanish and Arabic – was set up in 2005. It was always intended to give a Russian slant to global news reporting in response to the seemingly hegemonic Western-centric reporting of major international networks such as CNN and the BBC. Although decried by many from the start as simply propaganda, its content in the first few years of broadcasting had a bias – as news organisations invariably do – but was wise enough to allow for nuance, disagreement and intelligent discussion. The 'view from Russia' aspect came as much from the selection of news stories as from any dull propagandist commentary. Those who watched the channel in the West did so on account of its enabling viewers to find out about newsworthy events around the world that were not, or scarcely, covered by the dominant Western networks. For example, if a British viewer wanted to watch coverage of the massive demonstrations against Georgia's President Saakashvili in autumn 2007, it was no good watching the BBC, as they were barely mentioned. RT was the go-to channel in that case. But RT changed and, as an editor told the *Moscow Times* in 2010, 'started being really provocative'. Such provocation has meant an increasingly anti-Western stance. In practice this entails, alongside fairly standard coverage of news, such content as giving a platform for little-known US-based 'experts' – often on a dodgy Skype feed from their homes – to show that even Americans decry their country's policies, along with allocating air-time to activists taking positions in line with Russian policy and reporting on domestic news in the country of broadcast so as to emphasise that country's shortcomings.

As the blurb of a regular RT programme in the UK has it, the aim is to 'go underground to discover the stories that aren't being covered by the mainstream media', with the opening voice-over declaring:

> when lawmakers manufacture consent instead of public wealth, when the ruling classes protect only themselves, when the financial merry-go-round lifts only the one percent up, it's time to ignore middle-of-the-road signals – going underground to bring real news to Britain and the world.

It is fair enough, up to a point. But in wider terms, this is no longer simply a Russian voice in a global conversation. It's shouting across the room in an attempt to drown out and countermand what your opposite number is shouting back. To those whose preference is for give-and-take, nuance and balanced consideration of issues, such an approach seems tremendously retrograde – a step back to the style of Cold War propaganda. On the other hand, it is also – sadly – very up-to-date and in keeping with the move towards echo-chamber polarisation that has come to dominate much political debate in the West during the second decade of this century.

RT has no monopoly on the preference for a party line over more balanced reporting and analysis. Where it does differ from the other major players in the world of international news networks is with regard to its reliance on state funding. The UK broadcast regulator Ofcom has investigated the reporting of RT, particularly in relation to coverage of the conflicts in Syria and Ukraine in 2014. The regulator found RT to be in breach of aspects of broadcast standards in relation to impartiality and misrepresentation, and as a result RT withdrew a programme from its roster and its website. For the sake of context, though, it should be noted that Ofcom regularly adjudicates on whether broadcasters are in breach of regulations. In the same Ofcom Bulletin that found RT to have fallen short of expected standards, cases concerning broadcasting standards were also upheld against both Fox News and Channel Five.

Nor should the impression be given that RT is either constantly in breach of regulations, or is the only viewpoint on global news coming out of Russia. There is a range of viewpoints in the Russian media with some far more vehemently anti-Western than RT and some more objective. Where RT stands out, though, is in its role as an international news platform broadcasting in several languages across the world, with a global reach of over 700 million people in more than 100 countries. At a gala dinner to celebrate RT's tenth anniversary in December 2015, President Putin tried to tread a line between asserting that, despite its funding, RT was editorially independent, free and not in the business of creating blunt propaganda in the service of the Russian authorities, while at the same time noting that it was RT that had explained 'the real events' in Ukraine and that 'yes, of course, you broadcast our point of view on practically all questions'.

RUSSIAN CIVILISATION, IDEOLOGY AND THE IZBORSKY CLUB

In 2012, a gathering of some of the most prominent anti-Western, anti-liberal figures in Russia took place in the small town of Izborsk, an ancient settlement marked by a stone fortress in the far west of Russia, nudging up to the border with Estonia. Here they established a group-cum-think tank called the Izborsky Club, an expert group made up of some of the best-known names in Russian patriotic politics. The permanent membership of this invitation-only political club consists of around thirty leading figures from across the socially conservative-statist spectrum. They describe themselves as encompassing a range 'from socialists and Soviet patriots to monarchists and Orthodox conservatives'. Some more critical Western observers prefer to designate the Izborsky Club as an intellectual circle situated on the extreme right of Russia's political spectrum. Chaired by veteran nationalist author, campaigner and editor of the far-right daily *Zavtra* ('Tomorrow') Alexander Prokhanov, its membership includes such well-known figures as Eurasianist ideologue and sometime Moscow State University professor Alexander Dugin, Orthodox priest and bestselling author Archimandrite Tikhon and economist, politician and adviser to President Putin, Sergey Glazyev.

The timing of the Izborsky Club's foundation was auspicious, coming as it did a matter of months after Vladimir

Putin reclaimed the presidency from his placeholder Dmitry Medvedev. With semi-official backing, the newly established Club achieved immediate prominence, as its ideologically driven analyses chimed with the increasingly conservative, statist and Eurasianist tone of Vladimir Putin's third term as Russian President (2012–2018). The Izborsky Club's first analytical reports included warnings that 'a series of regional armed conflicts close to Russia's borders' were likely to soon arise. When such conflicts came, with the annexation of Crimea and fighting in southern and eastern Ukraine in 2014, both the stock and the rhetoric of the Izborsky Club appeared to rise. While always being at one remove from the President's inner circle, the writers and ideologues of the Izborsky Club now seemed to be in line with and useful to the regime. Putin and the Russian regime in general had long seemed to many members of the Izborsky Club to be too liberal and guilty of buying into excessively Western approaches to politics and economics. The Izborsky Club does not have a precisely defined ideology. Its membership includes several writers and thinkers whose works span many years, hundreds of volumes and millions of words. On the margins during the 1990s, these men – and one woman, the historian Nataliya Narochnitskaya – are well used to expressing themselves independently and forcefully. Their standpoints, forms of expression and areas of expertise vary sufficiently to scupper any pretensions that some grand programmatic statement might emerge from the Izborsky Club. And yet, the members of the Izborsky Club have enough in common to create an identifiable sense of what they stand for; in short, the greatness and superiority of Russian civilisation and the correspondingly defective and inferior nature of the West.

In terms of its view of Russia, the Izborsky Club – like Putin from his 'Millennium Manifesto' onwards – favours an eclectic approach. Some members laud the Soviet Union's prosaic combination of superpower status and military might, egalitarian socialism and the urban proletariat, the might of industrial machines and the scientific-technical revolution. Others embrace a more poetic conceptualisation, drawing on Imperial Russia and the traditions of Russian Orthodoxy, pastoral visions of peasant villages and the expanse of the steppe, wooden churches and birch tree forests. The writings of the Izborsky Club often draw together the Red and White streams of Russian identity that clashed brutally in the post-revolutionary Civil War of 1919–1921. Alexander Prokhanov, the Club's founder, has been explicit in making such a drawing together central to their approach and noting that this is in line with President Putin's intention.

In January 2012, during what passed for a presidential election campaign in Russia, Putin published an article in a national paper, *Nezavisimaya gazeta*, on the subject of national culture. He asserted that:

In our country, where in many people's heads the civil war has not yet ended and where the past is extremely politicised and 'torn up' into ideological quotations (often interpreted by different people in directly opposing ways), subtle cultural therapy is needed. A cultural policy that on all levels – from school materials to historical documentaries – would form such an understanding of the unity of the historical process in which a representative of each ethnic group, just like any descendant of a 'Red commissar' or a 'White officer', would see his place. He would feel himself to be an heir of the 'one for all' idea – of the contradictory, tragic, but great history of Russia. We need a strategy for national policy based on civic patriotism. Any person living in our country must not forget about his faith and ethnic affiliation. But he must above all be a citizen of Russia and be proud of that.

In terms of its view of the West, the Izborsky Club needs a declining and dissolute West to facilitate its civilisational discourse of Russian superiority. Its members' writing does not, however, promote Russian isolationism, as they pointedly admire other non-Western civilisations and powers; for example, holding a meeting with former Iranian President Mahmoud Ahmadinejad, renowned even more than most Iranian politicians for the vehemence of his condemnation of the United States. The picture of the West, and particularly the Anglo-Saxon West, painted by the Izborsky Club and their ilk carries echoes of the old Soviet Communist Party mantra about the inevitability of the collapse of capitalism. Western authors who question the excesses of global capital are quoted approvingly. The West is seen as a civilisation in economic, moral and spiritual decline.

The Red–White amalgam of the Izborsky Club can be vague in detail but is vivid in symbolism. The members of the Izborsky Club churn out thousands of words a month published in a glossy full-colour A4-sized magazine, never less than 100 pages in length, called *Russian Strategies*. Note the plurality of the title; within the broad civilisational anti-Westernism of the Club, several streams come together. The full-colour glossiness of the monthly *Russian Strategies* magazine speaks not just of the resources backing the venture, but also of the fact that the pictures and symbols matter as much if not more than the words. Each issue, even almost each page, contains magnificent photographs, collages and artwork: figures from Russian and Soviet history, old black-and-white photographs, paintings in the classical style of Imperial cavalry regiments during the Patriotic War against Napoleon's grande armée, stark socialist-realist monuments of muscled Soviet workers hewn from granite, headscarf-wearing wrinkled peasant women smiling from their wooden porches, eagles soaring over snow-capped mountains, cosmonauts in training, onion-domed churches, scientists in spotless laboratories, forests, factories, Orthodox priests, breath-taking landscapes, bridges, rivers, maps, satellite images, icons and on and on in a series of pictures that create an idealised gallery of Russia.

These images draw together the streams of rural tradition and scientific progress, spirituality and economic strategy. Not atypically, the first issue of 2017 contains among its many illustrations a painting of the Soviet dictator Josef Stalin standing in a room next to a thick red curtain and beneath a golden icon of Christ, seated next to him is the figure of the Virgin Mary in the garb of a Russian peasant woman, through the window to the left of the picture are the colourful domes of St Basil's Cathedral. The picture illustrates an article on 'the role of I. V. Stalin in re-establishing the rights of the Russian Orthodox Church'. In each issue, the themes recur. Here's a quick comparison of the contents pages of the first ever issue in 2013 with issue one of 2017: both have sections on Russian civilisation under threat, on the Western challenge to Russia, on the spiritual security of the Russian world, on the significance of education and scientific advancement and on the importance of mobilising the Russian people. They're nothing if not consistent.

PUTIN THE CONSERVATIVE POPULIST

The extraordinary work of the Izborsky Club can, if taken on its own, seem a little overwhelming and even frightening in its determined anti-Westernism, militarism and relentless urgings to defend and expand Russian influence. The key question, of course, is how seriously this needs to be taken. Do the fulminations of such figures represent the views of Russia's ruling regime or of the Russian people more widely? Is it really the case that leading Izborsky Club member Alexander Dugin can be reliably referred to, as a headline carried by the US journal *Foreign Affairs* in 2014 had it, as 'Putin's Brain'? The answer, in short, is that the ideas coming out of the Izborsky Club are worthy of noting but not of inflating with regard to their importance to Russia's policy-makers. There is no doubt that this rebirth of emphasis on Russian civilisation, its history, culture and achievements resonates strongly with a good proportion of the patriotic Russian people. The vague sense of vague threat from the vague entity called 'the West' represents a reality for many Russians, and particularly so as it has been fostered by their rulers in recent years and enjoys a strong presence in the popular media. The rise of the Izborsky Club coincided – but not, as it were, coincidentally – with the conservative turn of Putin's third term from 2012 onwards. Its ideological position proved particularly pertinent to the regime's needs as the annexation of Crimea signalled a definitive anti-Western move marked by the rhetoric of military strength, Russian and Soviet history and civilisational identity. The Russian regime and those close to it increasingly spoke in terms similar to the Izborsky Club about aspects of Western decline. A moral front was opened up, with the unfortunate moniker 'gayropa' becoming an internet meme among conservative Russians seeking to single out European tolerance surrounding sexuality as a symbol of moral decline that encapsulates wider social signs of civilisational collapse.

As his third term began, President Putin expressly positioned himself as a conservative global leader, declaring in his annual address to parliament in 2013 that, 'in the words of Nikolai Berdyaev [Russian philosopher, 1874–1948], the point of conservatism is not that it prevents movement forward and upward, but that it prevents movement backward and downward, into chaotic darkness and a return to a primitive state.' He warmed to his theme still further a year later, promoting 'fundamental conservative values such as patriotism and respect for the history, traditions and culture of one's country' while regretting that 'for some European countries, national pride is a long-forgotten concept and sovereignty is too much of a luxury'.

Observing the admiration for Vladimir Putin that has been evident among nationalist politicians in Europe and the United States – for example, ex-UKIP leader Nigel Farage in Britain, French presidential runner-up Marine Le Pen and, of course, President Donald Trump in the United States – those who only see Russia through the prism of international relations puzzle at the apparent contradiction of these nationalist politicians admiring the leader of a country that appears to oppose the foreign policies of their own homelands. The explanation lies in a shared social conservatism. For all the differences that Western political figures have with Vladimir Putin in relation to foreign policy and democratic practice, Russia's President knows that his 2013 assertion that many people in the world 'support our position on defending traditional values' is not without foundation and represents an area of discourse that is both more fruitful and less specific than engagement over intractable international issues.

THE IDEOLOGY OF A NON-IDEOLOGICAL REGIME

The ideological key to understanding what goes on inside Russia's domestic politics has remained consistent, certainly since Vladimir Putin came to the presidency in 2000, and indeed can be seen emerging during the Yeltsin presidency in the 1990s. It is patriotic unity. As noted in Chapter Two, all three of Russia's post-Soviet Presidents have been reluctant to engage in divisive party politics, preferring to position the presidency as in some sense above politics and themselves as President for all Russians. When they have felt obliged to create parties in order for the political system to function, both Yeltsin and Putin hit upon names for those parties that emphasise their catch-all nature – Our Home Is Russia, Unity, United Russia. Just as President Putin is reluctant to tie himself too closely to any particular faction in terms of personnel policy, so he and his regime retain some flexibility in ideological terms. While content to identify themselves as conservatives and patriots in the broadly defined cultural terms discussed in this chapter, it is a step too far to talk of an ideologue from the Izborsky Club as 'Putin's brain'. For all their easy symbolism and useful overlap with regime positions, particularly post-Crimea, the members of the Izborsky Club have little popular or policy purchase when it comes to detailed proposals. Their programmatic positions tend to be outside the mainstream of regime thinking. For example, it does not enhance our understanding of the Kremlin's position on the conflict in Ukraine to take too seriously the assertion of leading Izborsky Club member and one-time Putin adviser Sergey Glazyev in 2014, that Ukraine has been occupied by the United States in order to militarise the population behind a Nazi regime that intends to invade Russia and start a World War. The patriotic conservatism of Russia's ruling regime, linked to a particular conceptualisation of Russian civilisation and its place in the contemporary world, presents sufficient problems for global peace and international relations as it is – even with far more sober voices than Mr Glazyev's determining future policies.

Nor is the Izborsky Club the only club or think tank in play in Kremlin circles. Once a year there is a meeting of the Valdai Discussion Club, usually addressed by Russia's President, at which specialists on Russia from around the world – many of whom are highly critical of the Russian regime and its policies – present papers, hold discussions and freely question Russia's President and other leading politicians. Before 2012, during the presidency of Dmitry Medvedev, the think tank that was closest to the Kremlin was a somewhat liberal reformist group, the Institute of Contemporary Development, with the President as the Chair of its Board of Trustees. That particular body has very much disappeared from the scene since Putin returned to the presidency. The national unity so dear to Russia's governing establishment, however, requires some degree of flexibility and latitude if it is to command support across a sufficiently broad section of political actors in the population. In his presidential addresses of 2015 and 2016, Vladimir Putin adopted an approach which is rhetorically dull in comparison with the national-patriotic declamations of, for example, the Crimea Speech in March 2014. Nevertheless, the bottom line in terms of Russia's formal positioning received emphasis by repetition in the President's 2016 address to parliament. Twice Vladimir Putin asserted that:

Our citizens have united around patriotic values, not because they are satisfied with everything, no, they have enough difficulties and problems. But they understand the reasons for these, and have a firm assurance that together we will overcome them … no matter what side of the barricades our forebears were on. Let's remember that we are a single people, a united people, and we have only one Russia.

CHAPTER EIGHT

RUSSIA IN THE WORLD

THE STRANGE FOCUS ON WHAT HASN'T HAPPENED

'The war with Russia began in Ukraine in March 2014', so declared former British General Sir Richard Shirreff in 2016. If anyone would recognise war, you would think that it might be a senior British General. After all, before his retirement from the military, Shirreff served as NATO's Deputy Supreme Allied Commander Europe between 2011 and 2014. But despite his qualifications, Sir Richard is, in the most straightforward sense, wrong. It seems unnecessary to state it, but let us be clear from the outset of this chapter: Britain has not been at war with Russia since 2014. There may be room for different takes on the relationship between the United Kingdom and Russia, as with the wider relationship between 'the West' and Russia, but there is no room here for hyperbole.

Shirreff's assertion comes from his real-world preface to a work of fiction, a novel that bears the provocative title *2017:*

War With Russia. The General, now released from the re-
straining regulations and responsibilities of high command,
has the freedom to pen fictional warnings of invasion, military conflict and general slaughter in the form of 'future
history'. At around the same time as Shirreff's book was published, he participated in a BBC 'mockumentary' alongside a
host of other retired British security, diplomatic and military
luminaries conducting a 'war game' where Russian military involvement in Latvia and Estonia threatens nuclear
war. You can play this 'game' yourself on the BBC's 'Could
you Stop World War Three?' website, which helpfully sets
out five steps to Armageddon.

Shirreff and the BBC join an eager group of international comrades in inventing fictional scenarios based on
Russian military expansionism. In Norway, the gripping
drama series *Occupied* (2015), based on an idea from crime
writer Jo Nesbø, told the near-future tale of the European
Union and Russia agreeing that Russian troops should take
control of Norway's oil fields and eventually – here lies the
dramatic tension – much more. So successful was this series
that a second season has been made. Russia's ambassador to
Norway, Vyacheslav Pavlovsky, displayed less enthusiasm for
Occupied than its audience, expressing concern lest anyone
actually think that this TV drama represents an accurate
portrayal of Russian intentions and so serves 'to scare Nor-
wegian viewers with the non-existent threat from the east'.
The situation is little better in Russia, where a browse along

the shelves in Moscow's bookstores reveals title after title reinforcing the alleged chasm between East and West. Swiss politician Guy Mettan's book on Russophobia, *Russia and the West: A Thousand Year War* (2015), has been translated into Russian, complete with the front cover strapline 'Why we love to hate Russia'. And there are plenty of Russian authors willing to stir up more antagonism. Titles such as Igor Prokopenko's *Evil Myths about Russia: what they say about us in the West* (2016) sit alongside the series *Russia: Enemies and Friends*, including the titles *England's Plot Against Russia* (2015) and *How the USA Devours Other Countries in the World: Who's Next? Russia?* (2015).

The very existence of such books, television programmes and countless online postings embracing similar ontologically combative conceptualisations confers substance on the fears and antagonisms that they contain. An iterative process between popular mood and media output feeds into the creation of friend and foe images, and – as any constructivist International Relations theorist would argue – into the conduct of international relations and the process of policy development itself. Some theorists make the case that where a country's élite propagates such divisive enemy images of other states, it is responding to pre-existing popular conceptualisations. Others – the majority – would pin the blame more firmly on the élite itself for shaping the people's views and turning them against a perceived potential enemy.

INTERPRETING REAL EVENTS IN THE REAL WORLD

Of course, it would be foolish to argue that the potentially disastrous decline in relations between Russia and the West in the past decade stems entirely from reckless image creation and unwarranted scare-mongering. Real events in the real world play key roles, as we shall see in this chapter's discussion of, for example, NATO expansion and wars in Syria, Iraq, Serbia, Georgia and Ukraine. Nonetheless, perceptions and narratives matter. The prism through which a country is seen distorts assessments and shapes responses. When NATO expanded during the late 1990s and early 2000s, perhaps Russia could have chosen to see this as a reasonable and non-threatening process by which independent nations were strengthening their security. Instead, drawing on decades if not centuries of antagonistic relations with European powers, NATO expansion was interpreted in Moscow as an unwarranted movement by potential enemies onto its borders in negation of mutual understandings agreed at the end of the Cold War. When the Russian armed forces conduct exercises within Russia, these could be seen by NATO and Western states as the standard and legitimate military practice of a major power undertaken to keep their armed forces prepared for all eventualities. Instead, with decades of deployment to prevent Soviet expansionism behind it, NATO has seen such manoeuvres as – once again in the words of General Sir Richard Shirreff – a massive military build-up akin to the Russian wolf prowling around the flimsy fence of the Baltic chicken coop.

Interpretations of events are shaped by, and in turn shape, the language used when assessing those events. We live, for example, in an age where the epithet 'war' is thrown around freely. When discussing Russia, the terms 'information war' and 'cyber war' have become commonplace, as if propaganda and computer hacking in themselves equate to armed conflict. They do not. Influencing the media (both traditional and new) and infiltrating the information systems of an enemy with malware and spyware have their parts to play in modern warfare, but for these actions to be war requires them to take place during a war. On their own – absent armed forces killing the enemy in the field and, though this is far less in vogue than it used to be, declarations of war by the states concerned – they do not a war make. They may be undesirable and harmful, but they are not war.

And this matters because clarity and precision in language facilitate appropriate responses in international relations. At the same time as computer hacking and 'fake news' are misidentified as war, recent years have seen genuine armed conflict in Europe, with the active participation of the Russian state. During the short Russo-Georgian war of August 2008, the Russian army entered South Ossetia and Abkhazia – separatist regions of Georgia – in response to a forceful move by Georgian troops into South Ossetia. The shelling of residential areas, a build-up of civilian casualties and the deployment of Russian armed forces that were regaining confidence, competence and *matériel*; all of these served as brief but telling precursors for the far more substantial and longer lasting conflict in the Donbass region of Ukraine from 2014 onwards. Although the fighting in the Donbass does not formally pit the uniformed Russian military against the Ukrainian armed forces, there is no doubting Kremlin military support for the pro-Russian separatists of the region in their conflict with the Ukrainian state. Nor can the instigation of this war be separated from Russia's annexation of Crimea in March 2014.

In the three years following its commencement in March 2014, the war in the Donbass resulted in over 10,000 deaths. More than a quarter of these fatalities are civilian, and according to UN statistics at least 1.6 million inhabitants of the region were displaced from their homes over this same period. The Donbass conflict stands as a shocking blight on Europe's recent history. The fighting itself has been marked by indiscriminate shelling, repeated ceasefire violations, the persistent use of heavy weaponry and the widespread devastation of housing and infrastructure. Such stark physical carnage, however, has been accompanied in much of Western Europe by markedly muted media coverage. The fighting is not ignored, and the terrible tragedy of 298 deaths in the shooting down of Malaysia Airlines Flight MH17 over the region in July 2014 received the shocked attention due; nonetheless, that so devastating a war has continued in the heart of Europe for over three years and counting remains to impact on the wider European consciousness and conscience.

How do we explain these contemporary perspectives that magnify into warfare technological meddling and the peddling of misinformation, while walking by on the other side of actual shell-bursting conflict? There may be some exaggeration for effect in that question – not least because diplomatic efforts at brokering a resolution to war in the Donbass have continued under the auspices of the Organization for Security and Co-operation in Europe – but it nonetheless contains a truth at its heart. In the West, a huge amount of attention is paid to allegations of Russian wrongdoing internationally, from election meddling through to doping in sport, while the attention paid to a devastating war in the heart of Europe pales in comparison. In Russia, ubiquitous anti-Westernism accompanies most media reportage of international affairs, reflecting and reinforcing the positions of politicians and public alike. Some explanation for this state of affairs can be found through consideration of the narratives – or, to put it in more scholarly language, the hegemonic discourses – owned by opposing camps. The stories that we tell of how the world got to be as it is shape our understanding and decision-making when it comes to current events. Russia's account of international relations in the twenty-first century differs markedly from the dominant narrative in the West. To set out that account is not to endorse it, but rather to seek the titular goal of this volume and to get inside Russian politics.

THE CASE OF CRIMEA I: WHAT HAPPENED?

On Friday 28 February 2014, the international airport in Simferopol, the capital of Crimea, was taken over by unidentified soldiers. Over that weekend, more strategic objectives across Ukraine's Crimean peninsula began to be seized in so efficient a manner as to suggest that these men were not simply untrained local militia reacting to the political chaos engulfing the government in the Ukrainian capital, Kiev. The fighters wore military fatigues but no insignia, earning them the inappropriately anodyne sobriquet 'little green men'. A report on BBC television that first Sunday morning in March 2014 showed a roadblock that had been erected on a strategic main road in Crimea, preventing the reporter and film crew from progressing beyond it. The reporter's questions to the anonymous troops guarding these barriers went unanswered. *Daily Telegraph* Moscow correspondent Roland Oliphant had made his way to the Ukrainian army base in Perevalne, a few miles to the south-east of Simferopol. He could see 'hundreds of heavily armed Russian troops, with clips in their assault rifles and machine guns. They won't say what they are doing here, but they won't let us approach the entrance to the base.'

Back in the studio, Sir Paddy Ashdown – former High Representative for Bosnia and Herzegovina – talked in tones of deep concern: 'We are one pace away from catastrophe at the moment – it would require one foolish act, a trigger happy Russian soldier, a Ukrainian guard who acts aggressively at one of these institutions taken over by Russian supporters, a foolish act now could tip us over the edge.'

Despite the initial obfuscation, the central fact that would come to dominate Russia's international – and indeed domestic – politics over the coming years soon became apparent. Russia had taken part of another state, Ukraine, for its own by force.

So audacious and startling a move overturned previous assumptions of how contemporary Europe operates. On the Saturday of that crucial weekend, President Obama talked to President Putin for an hour and a half, expressing deep concern about Russia's violation of international law and Ukraine's territorial integrity, warning him in turn that Russia faced international isolation if it continued to act as it was doing. Media reports, fudging a little the complexities of the Yugoslav Civil War in the 1990s, talked of Russia's action being the first time that one European nation had seized territory from another since the end of the Second World War. After Crimea, everything changed for the worse in terms of Russia's relations with the West. From this military fait accompli stems Russia's ejection from its main Western-centric organisation, the G8. From this stems, to name but a few, economic sanctions against Russia and personal sanctions against a number of prominent Russians deemed to have played a role in Crimea's annexation, or in the subsequent fighting by Russia-backed separatists in south-eastern Ukraine; fears that Russia is once again following the expansionist path of its Imperial and Soviet predecessor states, and NATO's subsequent response in the form of sending reinforcements to Poland and the Baltic States; even the renewal of long-forgotten anxieties that the shadow of nuclear war looms still over the world (see Chapter Nine).

THE CASE OF CRIMEA II: OUR NARRATIVE, THEIR NARRATIVE

Few could argue with the preceding few paragraphs, since they seek to deal in facts alone, setting out what happened in Crimea in spring 2014 and what has happened to Russia's relations with the West since that time. But facts alone do not shape international relations. States also base their policies on what is said, what is understood and what is intended. Discourse and narrative matter. From this perspective, at best, facts in international relations morph swiftly from the objective to the subjective. What happens matters too, of course, but we see what happens through the prism of our interpretation. Two weeks after Russian troops took control of Crimea, US Secretary of State John Kerry met with Russian Foreign Minister Sergei Lavrov in London. It was a long meeting. Afterwards Kerry summed it up by saying that the two men 'talked for a good six hours and … really dug into all of Russia's perceptions, their narrative, our narrative, our perceptions and the differences between us'.

In 'their narrative' and 'our narrative', cold facts do not remain undisputed for long. From the Russian perspective, Crimea is not simply a part of Ukraine that Russia has annexed. Crimea's history is linked closely to Russian history. It has been under Moscow's rule for long periods of time, and it only ended up in Ukraine when the Soviet Union split up because in 1954 Soviet leader Nikita Khrushchev made the administrative decision to transfer jurisdiction of the territory within the single Soviet state from Russia to Ukraine. From the Russian perspective, a majority of the population of Crimea support integration with Russia and expressed this desire in a referendum on 16 March 2014 that could only be held because Moscow had gained control of the territory. From the Russian perspective, the location of the Russian navy's principal southern port in Sevastopol in Crimea meant that, under the terms of its agreement with the Ukrainian state to maintain that presence, up to 25,000 Russian military personnel were allowed to be based on the Crimean peninsula. Building on this, it was argued that the Crimean operation in 2014 had not been an invasion, but that the Russian troops deployed were present legitimately and their actions had been in support of the Crimean population's right to self-determination.

Furthermore, President Putin asserted that Russia acted in Crimea when it did because events in Ukraine represented a security threat to the Russian state. The overthrow of unpopular but democratically elected Ukrainian President Yanukovych in February 2014 – after months of violent demonstrations in Kiev and elsewhere – marked a victory for the 'Euromaidan' protesters* and their political supporters, who sought closer links with Western Europe rather than with Russia. The ouster of Yanukovych had been far from clean, with a diverse mishmash of political forces engaged in the protests, from optimistic pro-European democrats to far-right Ukrainian nationalists. To add to the anti-Russian mix, in December 2013 US Assistant Secretary of State

---

* 'Euromaidan' refers to the protesters' pro-European political position, and their physical position on Kiev's Maidan Nezalezhnosti (Independence Square).

Victoria Nuland visited Kiev, where she met protesters on Independence Square and reportedly handed out food to them. Seen through Russian eyes, the demonstrations that drove Yanukovych from office looked very much like another Western-backed removal of a pro-Russian head of state. The Association Agreement between Ukraine and the European Union, whose ratification was a central goal of the protesters, included stipulations that Ukraine would converge with EU security policies; and Russia saw this as a threat to its continued maintenance of the Sevastopol naval base.

THE BACK STORY I: HOW RUSSIA VIEWS THE WEST

The specifics of the Crimea case bring together multiple aspects of a narrative strand that had been developing within Russia's ruling regime for more than twenty years, predating Vladimir Putin's rise to power. From the collapse of the Soviet Union in 1991 onwards, in Moscow the Atlanticist line competed with the Eurasianist line. The Atlanticists saw Russia taking its place alongside the Western powers; perhaps, but not necessarily, within a reconfigured set of international institutions. The Eurasianists regarded alliance with the West with suspicion, seeing Russia as a distinctive great power with its own sphere of influence. According to the Russian narrative that came to dominate in Putin's third term as President from 2012 onwards, Russia's initial preference for working closely with the West had been repeatedly thwarted. The Atlanticist position of most of the Yeltsin years (1991–1999) ended when NATO bombed Russia's Serbian ally in 1999 and in that same year expanded its membership into Eastern Europe. President Putin's steps to support the United States after 9/11 and to prioritise relationships with Europe, and particularly the United Kingdom, in his first term (2000–2004) came up against what Russia considered to be the unnecessary and threatening further expansion of NATO and, to a lesser extent, the EU, into the Baltic States. Russia identified the hand of the West too in the 'colour revolutions' that saw popular demonstrations overthrow pro-Russian ruling regimes in Ukraine, Serbia and Georgia in the early years of this century.

In March 2009, US Secretary of State Hillary Clinton gave her Russian counterpart, Foreign Minister Sergei Lavrov, a somewhat bizarre gift. In front of the TV cameras at a summit meeting in Geneva, Clinton produced a small gift-wrapped box that looked as if it might contain an item of jewellery. Removing its lid herself, she produced from within it a mock-up of a red button, like those 'emergency stop' buttons found near potentially dangerous machinery. Except on this button, the two words written – one in English, one in Russian – were not 'emergency stop'. The English word was 'reset', a reference to the laudable US conviction that worsening relations with Russia were in need of recalibration. Over recent months the presidencies of the United States and Russia had been taken over, in the persons of Barack Obama and Dmitry Medvedev, by two forty-something former law lecturers with comparatively liberal images. As if to emphasise the significance of symbolism in international relations, this coincidence was deemed sufficient to offer a new start to US–Russian relations – hence the button with the word 'reset' on it. The other word on the button was supposed to say 'reset' in Russian. It didn't. Instead it said 'overcharge'. The inadvertent symbolism within this incompetent and rather patronising attempt at diplomacy sent out one clear, if unintended, message: we don't speak your language.

The flawed attempts to 'reset' US–Russian relations during the Medvedev presidency (2008–2012) came to a final crashing end with the Ukraine crisis of 2013 onwards, where Moscow again considered the United States and the European Union to have acted in concert in supporting the removal of a pro-Russian leader in Ukraine and undermining Russia's national security. As former British ambassador to Moscow, Sir Tony Brenton, put it in 2014 when referring to both the removal of President Yanukovych and US Assistant Secretary of State Victoria Nuland's visit to Kiev, 'Russia sees this as a result of Western meddling, and doesn't think that the West is acting fairly. It's not helpful that the leading US diplomat was seen on the Maidan handing out cookies to protesters.'

A central and recurring element of Russia's narrative when it comes to relations with the West is the concept of 'double standards', an accusation repeatedly thrown at Western powers – and at the United States in particular – over many years when they criticise Russian actions. From this point of view, for example, the Kremlin views the West's stated commitment to democracy promotion as a convenient cloak providing moral concealment for such actions as military action in the Middle East that it sees as having more to do with oil and power than with spreading democratic values and practice. When it suits the West – the Kremlin would say – that declared commitment to democracy is laid aside and the elected President of Ukraine can be overthrown by the contentious politics of the street with the support of the United States and the European Union. After March 2014, the Putin regime claimed that the West displayed double standards regarding the cases of Crimea and Kosovo. Moscow argued that Kosovo's secession from Serbia, supported by both a majority of Kosovans and by the Western powers, was comparable with Crimea's vote on leaving Ukraine and joining Russia that was vehemently condemned in the West.

THE BACK STORY II: HOW THE WEST VIEWS RUSSIA

There are, of course, plenty of counter-arguments to the Russian narrative set out in some detail above. NATO expansion, for example, can be framed instead as the legitimate choice of independent nations to join the security alliance of their choosing, and the idea that Russia should have a voice with regards to that choice as inappropriate. The Kosovo–Crimea comparison can be undermined by pointing out the differences between the cases: Kosovo became independent and was not absorbed into another state while under that state's military control. Similarly strong countervailing views to the Russian narrative can be made in case after case. But the intention here is not simply to argue for a relativism that shrugs its shoulders and declares both sides to be as bad as each other, which is the underlying proposition behind the Kremlin's 'double standard' accusations. Policies and actions ought rather to be judged on their merits within a widely accepted normative framework that prefers peace to war, democracy to authoritarianism and human freedoms to state repression. For as long as states judge their actions on the international stage according to the Leninist principle of '*kto kogo?*' – 'who will beat whom?' or, literally, 'who whom?' – then these higher principles can only suffer.

In much Western discourse, too, an unhelpful binary approach has prevailed in recent years, as relations with Russia are framed in terms of a new Cold War. The resurrection of the language of the Cold War ill serves our understanding of international affairs several decades after that phase in global history passed. We are no longer faced with a world dogmatically divided into the two camps of Communism and capitalism – China is rising along with other 'emerging powers' across the globe and Communism as ideology or ideal has left the world stage. These tectonic shifts in global affairs have released Russia from the fixed moorings of its Soviet incarnation. It is more nimble now; free to make alliances and change policies without having to adhere to an inflexible ideological worldview and without dragging with it the unwieldy behemoth of dozens of client states.

Such flexibility is evident in the fact that, only a few years back, Russia cooperated closely with Western powers in the 'war on terror'. As recently as 2012–2015, the Russian government allowed a NATO transit hub for military personnel and supplies to operate in the southern Russian city of Ulyanovsk, the birthplace of the founder of the Soviet state, Vladimir Ilyich Lenin. Russian foreign policy has gone through several phases in this century alone. On the other side of the divide, 'the West' as a coherent group opposing Russia is subject to modification too. In 2003, the leaders of Russia, France and Germany held a summit in St Petersburg, sharing concerns over the invasion of Iraq by a US-led coalition and mirroring a similar summit in the Azores a few weeks earlier involving the leaders of the United States, Britain and Spain. On that issue, as on a number of others, no simple East–West bifurcation existed. Dusting off out-dated Cold War stereotypes only distorts perspectives; what is needed is analysis based in contemporary realities.

BEYOND EAST AND WEST

Since 2016, a year that saw both the election of Donald Trump as US President and the decision by the people of the United Kingdom to leave the European Union, it has become something of a commonplace to talk of international relations being in a state of flux. In fact, these two events are but the latest manifestations of a shaking of global affairs as the twenty-first century has taken hold. The 'rise of China', the 2008 financial crisis and the shift in global economic power away from Western Europe, North America and Japan to fast-growing economies around the world – not just China and India, but Malaysia, Mexico, Nigeria, Turkey and several other states – all contribute to the rearranging of the international security architecture. To look at Russia and Russian foreign policy only through a Western lens is to misinterpret Moscow's position and perspective in global affairs. In the 1990s, Russia's invitation to join the G7 group of leading industrial countries represented a US- and UK-led move to include what was seen to be a democratising post-authoritarian global power into the existing international structures established by the leading Western nations during the Cold War. By the time Russia was suspended from the G8 in 2014 after the annexation of Crimea, Foreign Minister Sergei Lavrov shrugged it off as no big deal since that 21st-century innovation the G20, with its wider membership encompassing all continents, is now the place for international cooperation and decision-making.

Another 21st-century innovation of growing significance in terms of Russia's place in the world, and of the emerging world order, is the Shanghai Cooperation Organisation (SCO). Established in 2001, its leading players have been Russia and China, with post-Soviet Central Asian countries making up the rest of its original membership. By the time India and Pakistan signed up for the SCO at the Tashkent summit in 2016, the group could claim to represent over 40 per cent of the world's population. From the outset, the SCO had a security focus, taking a stance in opposition to what was seen as the growing Western predilection for 'humanitarian intervention'. Major military exercises involving the Russian and Chinese militaries have taken place on several occasions. Some observers see the SCO as a rival to NATO, although there is as yet nowhere near so tight a military structure with ideas such as joint command and mutual defence treaties not on the table.

Without downplaying the military and economic cooperation that the Shanghai Cooperation Organisation represents, much of its added value comes in the fact that it is not Western. It represents a collective rebuff to any idea that the established democracies and their post-Second World War/Cold War order of things has come out on top and can remain unchallenged in perpetuity. The West is excluded from annual SCO summits, and the SCO provides an alternative against which emerging powers can play-off the established order. Turkey, for example, not making the progress that it hoped for in terms of membership of the European Union, began in late 2016 to talk about a pivot to Eurasia. President Erdoğan floated the idea that his country might join the Shanghai Cooperation Organisation.

We noted in Chapter Five that when a Russian leader comes to power, two 'first visits' traditionally have symbolic significance – the first internal visit beyond the capital and the first trip abroad. When Vladimir Putin came to power in 2000, his first trip abroad was to London – a sign of his declared commitment that Russia was above all a European country that sought integration into European institutions and networks. Indeed, the particular choice of London was taken at the time to indicate a westwards orientation seeking close ties beyond Europe and across the Atlantic, as the United Kingdom represented a political and cultural bridge between the European Union and the United States. By the middle of the decade, the policy focus had relocated. In 2007 President Putin decisively marked this shift in an address to the Munich Conference on Security Policy. Here he attacked the United States for showing disdain for the basic principles of international law and, alluding to the US-led invasion of Iraq in 2003, for militarily overstepping its national borders without the support of the United Nations. Putin sought to present the United States, and not Russia, as out of step with 'normal' rules of international behaviour. In the post-Crimea period, he would use similar discursive tactics in representing Russia as upholding traditional European norms while Western Europe stepped along the path of decline.

By the time that Dmitry Medvedev became President of Russia in 2008, Russia's foreign policy position had moved markedly from that adhered to at the century's opening. It was no surprise then that Beijing was the destination for Medvedev's first foreign trip as President. Four years later, President Putin visited the Chinese capital shortly after his third-term inauguration. The honour was reciprocated in 2013 when new Chinese President Xi Jinping's first trip abroad was to Moscow. In terms of its international profile, Russia had – for the time being, at least – given up on improved relations with Europe and the United States and made a decisive shift towards Asia. China's significance to Russia stems from multiple factors: its rapid economic growth, its proximity to Russia, its geopolitical position in global terms, its embodiment of an alternative mode of development to liberal democracy and its potential significance as a future ally or enemy. The Sino-Russian partnership represents no deep mutual commitment to shared values, but a pragmatic engagement seeking to bolster mutual interests. Within the Shanghai Cooperation Organisation, Russia is able to work alongside China and India at the same time as maintaining its good relations with most of the post-Soviet states that it would like to keep within the Russian sphere of influence. Of those countries that were formerly part of the Soviet Union, Kazakhstan, Uzbekistan, Kyrgyzstan and Tajikistan are all member states of the SCO; Belarus is an 'observer state' of the SCO; and Armenia and Azerbaijan are 'dialogue part- ners' of the SCO.

REVERSING THE CATASTROPHE?

In April 2005, President Putin delivered his fifth address to the Russian parliament as President, which is effectively his annual 'state of the nation' address. If his speechwriters were looking for a catchphrase, a single brilliant idea that would resonate with the President's listeners across the nation, even across the world, then they certainly found it. 'The collapse of the Soviet Union', the President declared, 'was the greatest geopolitical catastrophe of the twentieth century'.

Or did he say that? Rarely have a politician's words been subject to such interpretation or even deliberate distortion as has happened in relation to those expressed by Vladimir Putin that day. In the decade and more since that speech, time and again newspapers and commentators have misquoted

Putin by leaving out the qualifying adjective 'geopolitical'. A swift search shows the *Washington Post, The Guardian,* the *New York Times, USA Today* – to name but a few – all asserting that Russia's President thinks the collapse of the Soviet Union was the 'greatest catastrophe of the twentieth century'; more catastrophic than two World Wars, than the holocaust, than millions of deaths in that bloody century's mass repressions and man-made famines. And it's not just the media; examples can be found of scholars and politicians similarly misquoting Putin. Cue a righteous anger that would have been understandable if the President had said what they said he said, accompanied by insinuations that Russia's leader intends to reverse that catastrophe.

But Putin did not say that. He referred rather to the geopolitical catastrophe caused to Russia and its citizens as the Soviet Union broke up into fifteen independent states, and 'tens of millions' of Russians found themselves overnight living abroad, when the day before they had been part of a single country. Since 2005, linguists have even debated whether 'the greatest' is the correct translation of what Putin said. The Kremlin's official English version of his speech renders the phrase as 'the collapse of the Soviet Union was a major geopolitical disaster of the century', which is a secure enough translation, and one that is markedly at odds with more sensationalist readings. For the sake of our discussion here, though, the point is that if one wants to identify the first priority for Russian foreign policy, it will not be found by looking west to the United States and Europe, nor by looking east to China and Asia; it will be found closer to home, in the post-Soviet space (excluding the Baltic States whose status as members of NATO and the European Union sets them apart).

From this perspective, the assertion made above that Russia's shifting foreign policy priorities can be discerned by observing the destinations of its Presidents' first trips abroad after elections requires a corrective. Presidential 'first trips' to the UK in 2000 and China in 2008 were indeed indicators of international precedence, but in fact every single post-Soviet President of Russia has first made an official visit to a former Soviet state before venturing further afield.* President Yeltsin went to Kazakhstan (1991) and Belarus (1996); President Putin to Belarus (2000), Ukraine (2004) and Belarus again (2012); President Medvedev to Kazakhstan (2008). Before all else, it is the near neighbourhood that matters to Russia. The use of military force in Georgia and Ukraine makes clear the precedence that the states of the former Soviet Union take. We cannot understand Russian foreign policy without grasping the perspective that these states with geographical and historical contiguity to Russia are of primary importance when it comes to existential matters of security and economics.

Just as the United States displays decisive concern with regard to the make-up of regimes across the Americas, and has done so since the Monroe Doctrine of the nineteenth

---

* In most cases such a visit came en route to the more distant destination.

century, so Russia sees itself as having long-term and legitimate interests vis-à-vis its neighbours. So consequential are affairs pertaining to them that Moscow deploys military force *in extremis*. The preference – indeed, in most cases, the expectation – however, is that most of these countries, excluding the Baltic States, align themselves with Russia out of mutual interest. In May 2014, just a couple of months after the annexation of Crimea, the Heads of State of Russia, Kazakhstan and Belarus signed the founding treaty of the Eurasian Economic Union (EEU). Modelled on the European Union, the EEU forms a 'single economic space' with free movement of goods, capital, people and services. Its regulations are overseen by a Commission made up of representatives from each member state, whose work focuses on increased integration. A single currency has been mooted, and since the establishment of the EEU, Armenia and Kyrgyzstan have become member states. Away from all discussion of 'great power' positioning, breaking from the West and pivoting to Asia, the EEU has significant potential for increasing the economic strength of its members, acting as a consolidated block in developing trade links with the lucrative Asian market and improving the standards of living of its citizens.

RUSSIA IN THE WORLD: A CONCLUDING CONCEPTUALISATION

We began this chapter by considering the dramatically different conceptualisations of Russia in the world as apparent in the standard Western and Russian narratives. Although the significance of discourse can be over-exaggerated when divorced from real-world events, the force of perspective in policy formation stands strong and decisive. From the middle of this century's first decade in particular, relations between Russia and the West can most accurately be portrayed not even as clashing narratives, but rather as passing narratives; perspectives that are so far apart and so entrenched that there is barely space to register the dissenting view of the other. Indeed, the mis-translated 'reset' button that Hillary Clinton presented to Sergei Lavrov functions as the perfect symbol of interlocutors speaking different languages.

Ironically, however, if East–West tensions are not to continue accelerating towards conflict, it is a reset of perception that is required. Such a reset might start by junking historical Cold War analogies that serve only to emphasise and deepen divides. Looking beyond specific policy differences – many of which it could be argued are symptoms rather than causes of mutual mistrust – the fundamental divisions of the Cold War years no longer exist. There is no two-camp world, no ideological struggle and no competition between alternative economic systems. None of which is to say that history cannot be a useful source of perspective; it is just a matter of the historical examples chosen. A more unifying analogy than those stemming from the Cold War is that of post-imperialism. While it certainly offers no justification for iniquitous policy, the loss of empire in the modern world repeatedly causes after-shocks. Former imperial powers, faced with dramatic declines in their international standing and seeking a new role in relation to those states over which they had ruled, have commonly found themselves engaged in dubious and unwise actions. In the years after the Second World War, as France and Britain adjusted to their loss of power and territory, they engaged in questionable military adventurism in Algeria and Suez respectively. A direct comparison of such regrettable conflicts with the war in the Donbass or the annexation of Crimea by Russia in 2014 would be unwise, since each case –whatever their similarities so far as the horrors of war are concerned – is defined by its own specific circumstances. The same could be said, however, with regard to other historical analogies for these cases, such as the annexation of the Sudetenland and the dangers of appeasement. Lessons from history can be selected to suit any stance.

As this chapter has demonstrated, the Russian Federation has, for more than a quarter of a century since the collapse of the Soviet Union, been seeking its place in the world. Moscow's Soviet-era territorial possessions represented the largest contiguous land empire in history. This empire was lost – in historical terms – in an instant. No one should be surprised then at the policy twists and strategy turns that have marked Russian foreign policy since that time. Integration, isolation and multi-polarity have all been tried. Whether Russia is now settling on the status of a resurgent 'great power' increasing its territory by force and intervening in conflicts – such as Syria (see Chapter One) – on the world stage is difficult to state with certainty. As the next chapter makes clear, forecasts of Russia's future are – like the vision of many a policymaker and commentator – frequently obfuscated by preconception. What is certain, though, is that Russia's current regime will not last forever, and that scene-shifting in global affairs will continue.

CHAPTER NINE

LOOKING TO THE FUTURE

FORECASTING RUSSIA'S DECLINE

Political forecasting, particularly in the short to medium term, is something of a mug's game; but that doesn't stop analyst after analyst, the present author included, from playing it. Glimpses into the future fascinate most people. They allow possibilities and prejudices to be freed from reliance on facts alone. Experts on politics and international affairs must pack prediction into their metaphorical toolbox before any engagement with the media, as even a brief listen to any current affairs radio interview confirms: 'So, how will Russia react? What will President Putin do now? What's the next step after Crimea?'

At Europe's leading academic conference for the study of Russia – held annually by the University of Helsinki's Aleksanteri Institute – partway through Vladimir Putin's third term as President (2012–2018), a panel was convened consisting of experts who had written a whole book on what will happen next in Russia, and what various aspects of Russian socio-political life will be like in a decade or so. Two of the panellists disagreed, one offering an 'optimistic' view and the other taking a more 'pessimistic' line. Under the former, President Putin and his regime would be removed from office within a couple of years. Under the latter, the collapse of the Putin regime would take a few years longer. Leaving aside the question of whether regime collapse would be seen as an optimistic scenario by most Russians (as our analysis in Chapter Six notes, it wouldn't), these predictions represent a fine example of 'wishful forecasting'. Think of what you would like to see happen, and put it out there as an expert forecast.

We see wishful forecasting in all walks of political life. If an election or referendum produces a result at odds with what a particular analyst or commentator thinks, prophecies of impending doom are bound to follow – particularly so in this world of echo-chamber social media, where our tendency to follow those like us serves only to reinforce our chosen views and to exclude or ridicule the opinions of the obviously wrong. Wishful forecasting about Russia has been widespread for decades and shows no sign of disappearing. The respected US journal *Foreign Affairs* published an article in early 2015 by veteran political science professor and Russia-watcher Alexander Motyl, whose family background is Ukrainian and includes relatives killed by the Soviet authorities. It is safe to say that Motyl, for perhaps better reason than many, does not wish the Putin regime well – and it shows.

His piece bore the title 'Goodbye Putin: why the President's days are numbered'. A year later the same journal published another article by the same expert, but this one was called 'Lights out for the Putin regime: the coming Russian collapse'. These dramatic predictions of sweeping and elemental change are not uncommon when it comes to analysis of Russia. In summer 2016, US think tank the Jamestown Foundation launched its 'special project' on Russian affairs and gave it the title 'Russia in Decline', despite it coinciding with the re-emergence on the international stage of a strengthened and reinvigorated Russian state. Too often such prognostications seem to be conclusions searching for evidence, rather than deductions drawn from analysis of available data.

Contributions of this nature to the task of considering Russia's future represent what the former Moscow bureau chief of *Business Week*, Paul Starobin, termed Russia-is-doomed syndrome, as he accused the US media of possessing an 'unbalanced mind-set' and of having repeatedly 'chronically misdiagnosed' Russia. Starobin noted a tendency for analysts to inflate or distort factors that support their preferred future and to downplay those that do not. We have noted in Chapters Four and Six, for example, that the understandable affinity that Russian oppositionists who favour Western-style liberal democracy have with the Western media and public more widely has led to an exaggerated impression of their importance inside Russian politics. Acknowledgement of potentially distorting factors is important because forecasting is not simply a matter of intellectual game-playing. The prevailing views of influential people shape both long-term policy approaches and short-term reactions to events.

The point here is not to crow over failures in forecasting; after all, it is far easier to find these than to identify accurate predictions. At issue rather is the propensity noted throughout this volume for many observers of Russian affairs to routinely approach Russia as something 'other', so alien to our understanding that it is easier to predict its imminent demise and dramatic collapse than to work out a more realistic future path for its development. Browsing in a library a few months after the annexation of Crimea by Russia in 2014, I came across a notable example of the wishful forecasting tendency. Written by a journalist with considerable experience as a Moscow correspondent, it pointed to a ratcheting up of authoritarianism in Russia over the preceding year or so. It noted that a few of those who had taken to the streets to protest against the authorities had been arrested and sentenced to terms of imprisonment. It noted also a fall in living standards as imported goods became scarcer and Russian consumers, who could no longer so easily buy what they used to, became more dissatisfied. Its conclusion was that Russia found itself in a pre-revolutionary period. The precise timing of the regime's coming fall, it argued, was difficult to discern; it might be a matter of years or, possibly, much earlier, given the right spark in the form of a particularly pivotal event, such as a border war or unrest in a Moscow market. That forecast was written about Brezhnev's Soviet Union in 1969 (*The New Russian Tragedy* by Anatole Shub).

The pre-revolutionary period that Shub discerned had another couple of decades to go. Amidst many forecasters' presaging of regime collapse in relation to Russia today, the Brezhnevite scenario seems strangely absent. Leonid Brezhnev led the Soviet Union between 1964 and 1982, presiding over a period that Mikhail Gorbachev (Soviet leader 1985–1991) labelled 'stagnation'. These years seemed to go on and on with the same people in charge, a dominant conservative – albeit formally Marxist–Leninist – mind-set propagated by the state, consistent harassment of dissidents and a foreign policy that swung from détente with the West to the brink of nuclear conflict, and included incursions into states deemed to be within the Soviet sphere of influence. Such a Brezhnevite scenario today would see a relatively stable Russia – marked by a corrupt élite, high military spending, exposure to oil prices and an increasing cynicism among the public concerning the story which officials and the mainstream media tell – muddling through economic difficulties while focusing national pride on its ability to influence affairs on the world stage. This stability scenario may not be as exciting as the alternatives of collapse or even rebirth, but given that Vladimir Putin's mantra for the vast majority of his presidency has been stability – a Brezhnevite objective *par excellence* – it seems more likely than either of those alternatives. We may not like a good deal that Russia's ruling regime does, either domestically or internationally; but weakly founded assertions that it is tottering on the brink of collapse represent wishful forecasting that flies in the face of hard data, historical experience and rigorous consideration of the steps that might lead to such an outcome.

FORECASTING THROUGH THE PRISM OF RUSSIA'S RELATIONS WITH THE WEST

The Doomsday Clock, thought up by the Bulletin of the Atomic Scientists in 1947, has become a staple of the news media in the seven decades or so since then. Its premise is that it serves as a warning to the people of the world and their leaders of approaching nuclear annihilation. On the Doomsday Clock, Armageddon takes place at midnight, and the scientific community behind the Clock assesses human-kind's proximity to that apocalyptic event in terms of minutes to midnight. It goes without saying that measuring the immediacy of the apocalypse is an imprecise art. Nonetheless, the Doomsday Clock seeks to reflect techno-logical and scientific trends and to make judgements about leadership capacity in major nations, rather than to nudge its hypothetical minute hand forwards or backwards in regular reaction to temporary crises. This being the case, the closest that it has come to midnight was not during the Cuban Missile Crisis of 1962 when it stood at seven minutes to, before – presumably out of sheer relief – falling back to thirteen minutes to in 1963. The closest the Doomsday Clock came to midnight was rather in 1953, as the United States and the Soviet Union ploughed ahead with the production of hydrogen bombs. At that time the Bulletin ominously pro-nounced that all that was required was 'a few more swings of the pendulum, and, from Moscow to Chicago, atomic explosions will strike midnight'. By the time that the Soviet Union had collapsed in 1991 we could sit back, smiling in wonder at how we had arrived at seventeen minutes to world's end. By 2017 the Science and Security Board of the Bulletin had moved the minute hand of Doomsday forward to stand at two and a half minutes to midnight.

Two and a half minutes to midnight? Is that really where the world stands in 2017? Certainly in terms of the state of Russia's dealings with the West, this putative proximity to mutually assured destruction seems overstated. If we compare actual policy differences today with those between the Soviet Union and the United States during the Cold War, they are – although significant – of a notably lower order. It should be observed of course that relations between Russia and the United States are no longer the only factor taken into consideration in the positioning of the Doomsday Clock's minute hand – events on the Korean peninsula, for example, have their own destabilising impact. But the fact that between them Russia and the US possess around 90 per cent of the planet's nuclear weapons means that they continue to exert considerable influence on the Bulletin's estimates. Worsening relations with regard to military action in Ukraine and Syria contribute to the assessment, along with Russia's intention to develop new silo-based missiles and a new class of submarines carrying nuclear missiles, and US plans to modernise its air-, sea- and land-based missile capabilities. As argued in the preceding chapter, facts on the ground represent but one factor in international relations; the interpretation of these facts another. That the United States and Russia possess between them the capacity to destroy much of human civilisation several times over is a fact that we have lived with for decades. But that either side might be willing, or even preparing to do so dramatically changes the calculations.

In autumn 2016, the British press – tabloid and broadsheet alike – featured headlines such as 'Is Putin preparing for WW3? Russia begins evacuation of FORTY MILLION PEOPLE in huge drill' (the *Daily Express*), 'Russia launches massive nuclear war training exercise with "40 million people"' (*The Independent*), and 'BRACED FOR ARMAGEDDON. Terrifying footage shows Russian soldiers prepare for nuclear war during drill involving 40 million people' (*The Sun*). In terms of facts on the ground, such hysteria was wide of the mark. There was, of course, no evacuation of 40 million Russians – just think for a minute of the logistical impossibility and the implacable public outcry that would be involved in such a process. Nor even was there a huge drill focused on preparation for nuclear conflict. A brief scan of the website of Russia's Ministry for Emergency Situations – available in English for the benefit of UK journalists, and checked in Russian for the purposes of this paragraph – should have been enough for even the least intrepid investigative reporter to note that the focus of the exercise being carried out in Russia was not a putative nuclear conflict. It was the operation of the National Crisis Management Centre with particular reference to large disasters and fires. Vast wildfires have become in recent years a major issue in Russian political and public life, dating in particular from the devastating fires of 2010 and what was widely perceived to be an inadequate official response to them. Such fires have occurred most years since then and in the summer of 2016 seasonal fires were some of the worst on record. Greenpeace reported that they covered an astonishing 1 million hectares in Siberia. That Russia's Emergency Ministry should a few months later hold a major drill focusing on dealing with 'natural disasters' in the form of massive fires represents a normal response on the part of the Russian state; but the decision to include in this drill wider issues of 'technologically generated' disasters in the form of civil defence and radiation contamination meant that it was met with the sort of headline set out above.

Perceptions that the Russia state is actively preparing for a nuclear war cannot help but colour our views of Russia's future. Nor is there any shortage of journalists or politicians eager to reinforce these impressions. During the United Kingdom's general election in 2017, Defence Secretary Michael Fallon, keen to distinguish the Conservative Party's stance from that of the Labour Party, repeated his government's policy that Britain could not rule out first-strike use of its nuclear weapons. A minor Russian political figure with no role in Russia's government – a former military man and member of the upper chamber of the Russian parliament, Frants Klintsevich – noted Fallon's statement, expressed predictable concern that Russia would be the target of this first-strike policy and reinforced his self-declared tough response by asserting that were the UK to take on Russia in a nuclear conflict, Britain would be wiped out by a counter-strike as it is a comparatively small country. This unimportant and unsurprising statement hit the headlines in Britain, couched in terms of Russia's threat to raze the UK to the ground. There is a useful rule of thumb when it comes to interpreting international relations news stories in general; if they are based on statements from MPs with no executive role, they are not that significant.

Similar overstatement occurred in 2015 when Denmark agreed to fit some of its naval vessels with radars that would enable them to play a role in NATO's missile shield. Russia's ambassador to Denmark noted in a Danish newspaper that such a move would put these ships on Russia's nuclear target list. This military planning move was widely reported as Russia threatening to nuke Denmark if it took a role in NATO's missile shield, rather than as a decision to add such ships to a target list in case of future conflict. Since these media reports, military figures in the West have ventured the misleading assertion – based on a misreading of a poorly worded newspaper article by a relatively insignificant diplomat – that Russia has threatened to nuke Denmark.

The case of the Danish navy is illustrative. Facts on the ground caused tensions with Russia to rise and the interpretation of those facts raised the temperature still more. At the end of 2016, a YouGov survey in the United Kingdom reported that 57 per cent of the population consider World

War Three likely within the next forty years. A contemporaneous poll by the Levada organisation in Russia found that, when asked if in the future a war between Russia and NATO/United States is possible, only 10 per cent think that it is, while 77 per cent think not. So large a gap in perception prompts pause for thought as to why the majority of Britons see a Third World War looming in the coming decades, while the vast majority of Russians see superpower conflict as scarcely possible.

FICTION AND CONCEPTUALISATIONS OF THE FUTURE

It might seem surprising to some that Russians are more optimistic with regard to the prospect of avoiding global nuclear conflict than their British counterparts. After all, if any country has known the reality of catastrophe and suffering on a massive scale over the past 100 years, it is Russia. In today's Russia, the media are certainly not averse to portraying NATO and the West as an active threat. The shelves of Moscow's bookstores carry the occasional Russian versions of the sort of Third World War scenario fiction made popular in the West by the likes of Tom Clancy, Sir Richard Shirreff and – during the height of such fears in the early 1980s – Sir John Hackett. Popular fiction can provide an insight into the way people are thinking of the future, and indeed serious policy analysts have long been familiar with the process of penning fictional future scenarios in an attempt to plan present policy. Russia's annexation of Crimea in 2014 took politicians and Russia-watchers the world over by surprise, but such an event made up the plot of Tom Clancy's last, and posthumously published, novel, *Command Authority* (co-authored with Mark Greaney). This came out in 2013 and envisaged Russia easily taking over Crimea with scarcely a shot fired, presenting a fait accompli to the West before tentatively testing the military possibilities of further territorial gain in south-eastern Ukraine. After which, Clancy's and Greaney's 2013 account continued, Russia would decide that the costs of further incursion into Ukraine were too high and so withdraw, but nonetheless gain great kudos at home for reincorporating Crimea into the Russian Federation. *Command Authority* proved remarkably prescient.

Fictional accounts of the future represent a fairly common genre within Russian literature, and tend towards the dystopian. Dmitry Bykov's novel *Living Souls* (2006) portrays a mid-21st-century Russia that 'has lost its influence and descended into a farcical Civil War with an extreme right wing cult in power'. Vladimir Sorokin took a not dissimilar view in *Day of the Oprichnik*, also published in 2006, which saw Russia in 2025 as a country ruled over by a revamped, and suitably technologically advanced, version of Ivan the Terrible's palace guard. More commercially successful than either of these literary works is the post-apocalyptic dystopian series of *Metro* thrillers by Dmitry Glukhovsky, set in the 2030s in the Moscow underground system where all the survivors of a nuclear holocaust are forced to live in order to avoid the radiation above ground. Reflecting the divisions of Russia's history, the metro system is divided into belligerent groups representing, for example, the Communists, the Russian nationalists and the liberal marketeers. Glukhovsky's bestseller even spawned a successful video game.

Such dystopian visions of the future, however, are entertainment rather than forecast. Analysts at the state-backed Russian International Affairs Council (RIAC) – Moscow's equivalent of London's Royal Institute of International Affairs, Chatham House – explicitly reject either dystopian or utopian visions in their 'World in 100 Years' programme, although the programme's leader is a fan of American science fiction writer Ray Bradbury and, in particular, his short story *The Toynbee Convector*. In this tale, Bradbury tells of the inventor of a time machine who won fame when he returned from a trip 100 years into the future to report the paradise that his country was to become. A century later, nearing his death and content that the bright future had now arrived, Toynbee the inventor reveals that his time-travelling was a fraud; but a fraud with a purpose. So tired had he been of endless miserable predictions and despair for the future, of present attitudes where everyone 'would be gloomily satisfied that their predictions of doom were right from day one', that he decided to subvert these self-fulfilling prophecies of disaster and convince everybody of their bright future.

The RIAC's conjectures for 100 years from now are a little less positive than Toynbee's, but they do provide a reasoned middle-way between paradise and apocalypse, and base themselves on consultation with fifty experts across Russia's business, scientific, military, economic, medical and artistic sectors, and on the extrapolation of current trends. The project concludes that 'to act in concert and avoid confrontation will be critical both for Russia and for the whole world'; a little Pollyannaish, no doubt, and ripe for sniping at by those who focus on a Russian state taking almost diametrically opposed policy options in recent years. Nonetheless, a central contention of this chapter is that when considering Russia's future, we should not mistake today for forever. As we will shortly explore, although not predictable in a detailed and precise sense, there are trends in Russia's history that return again and again. Vladimir Putin will not be President forever, the nature of Russia's ruling regime will change as a new generation inevitably comes to power and Russia's future – as that of any nation – will be subject to global socio-economic, political and scientific developments.

RUSSIANS' CONCEPTUALISATIONS OF THE FUTURE

We have considered how some of Russia's writers and policy analysts envisage the future. What about the population at large? The Levada Center asked its respondents a series of future-oriented questions in December 2016, as it has done every year since 2006. The general trend over that decade is for gradually increasing optimism when it comes to avoiding disasters such as 'major technical catastrophes' or epidemics, with the majority now seeing these as unlikely. The vast majority (80 per cent in both 2006 and 2016) see a putsch to change the ruling regime as improbable, and more than two thirds in 2016 thought the same when it came to the possibility of mass demonstrations or ethnic conflicts occurring in Russia. Perhaps surprisingly, slightly fewer people today than ten years ago consider war with Russia's neighbouring states to be likely (25 per cent in 2006, 21 per cent in 2016). In a question that allows comparisons right back to 2003, the 2016 survey revealed a higher score than in any of these preceding years with regard to whether Russians were approaching the coming year with hope or not – 57 per cent of Russians took this optimistic stance in relation to 2017. It seems that most Russians do not see themselves as living in a country in decline.

THE RUSSIAN GOVERNMENT'S CONCEPTUALISATIONS OF THE FUTURE

In what to some extent seems like a cultural hangover from the Soviet Union's obsession with formulating five-year plans, the Russian government – as noted earlier in relation to such areas as cultural policy (Chapter Five) and the National Projects (Chapter Three) – regularly issues strategies, concepts, doctrines and so on, setting out goals and broad conceptualisations for the future in a range of different policy areas. Plans for the future in relation to Russia's ethnic groups, education, upbringing, the family, young people, information security, science and technology, patriotism, military education – all of these and more can be found set out in documents drawn up by their respective ministries. When it comes to visions of the future, the key documents that are analysed in most detail by international observers relate to the economy, security, defence and international affairs.

In May 2017, President Putin signed a decree approving Russia's National Economic Security Strategy until 2030, the headline focus of which is to emphasise the relationship between economic success and national security. Of particular interest to Western observers is Russia's bullish reaction to the punitive economic sanctions imposed on it by the United States and the European Union after the annexation of Crimea. This reaction amounts to a not entirely groundless celebration of Russia's response in terms of investing in its own technological, industrial and agricultural sectors with the aim of increasing self-sufficiency rather than reliance on international partners. Prime Minister Dmitry Medvedev has even, with a touch of sarcasm, thanked the West for imposing sanctions since they have led to counter-sanctions that function as a form of protectionism. The vision of Russia's future set out in the National Economic Security Strategy fits well with the trio of defence and international affairs related documents produced since 2014. December 2014 saw a new Military Doctrine, and this was followed a year later by a new Security Strategy, and another year on from that – in November 2016 – Russia's new Foreign Policy Concept was published. Taken together, these documents emphasise Russia's self-conceptualisation as a newly resurgent power, operating in an increasingly dangerous and volatile international situation and determined to play the role that it sees as befitting its status in the world.

Taking 2016's Foreign Policy Concept as the most recent statement of how Russia sees its place in the world over the coming years, one cannot help but be struck by the apparent inconsistencies of what is said, and what is intimated but left unsaid. There is the standard stated commitment to the rule of law and democracy that has marked Russian official statements ever since the Soviet collapse in 1991; though, obviously there is no reference to awkward matters such as the legal nihilism that even President Medvedev acknowledged in 2008, or the fact that post-Soviet Russian democracy will surely soon reach three decades of existence without a change of regime. Standard, too, is the commitment to the role of the United Nations – a commitment that came to the fore particularly in the years after 9/11 when Russia saw the United States as acting across the world without reference to the UN, on the Security Council of which Russia has a veto.

Most of the other goals that Russia sets itself over the coming decade speak to a self-conceptualisation as a great power regaining its due position on the global stage. The Foreign Policy Concept asserts Russia's role in protecting its citizens abroad, commits itself to the dissemination of Russian culture and language and promises to spread Russia's perspective across the world's media. The most chillingly double-edged pledge that the Russian state makes in its Foreign Policy Concept should be read in the light of the annexation of Crimea and the ongoing war in the Donbass: 'to pursue neighbourly relations with adjacent states, and assist them in eliminating existing – and preventing the emergence of new – hotbeds of tension and conflicts on their territory'.

WHAT WE KNOW ABOUT RUSSIA'S FUTURE

The future is constructed in our minds in a variety of ways. Wishful forecasting allows us to project our own convictions and ideas on the years ahead; to give them at least some form, if not substance, even though they may turn out to miss the mark in the long run. The more structured forecasts of analysts and think tanks deploy a range of techniques: building scenarios, consulting with experts and mapping the path of key drivers such as the economy, demographics and scientific developments. The popular mood has a tendency to judge the future more instinctively on the basis of the present, with improvements today making us more hopeful for tomorrow. Writers and filmmakers, artists and game designers – such creatives enjoy freer rein to play with the concept of the future. Occasionally even, their less guarded and bounded conceptualisations of what might come to pass actually do transpire. Just as there was scarcely a reasoned expert who predicted Russia's annexation of Crimea, but author Tom Clancy did, so, too, back in the 1980s analysts as a whole did not see the collapse of the Soviet Union coming, but Donald James's thriller *The Fall of the Russian Empire* (1982) made a fairly accurate stab at what was to unfold within the decade ahead. Forecasts in all of these varied forms are of a different – though related – genus from the way that those in power interact with the future. Governments are less interested in anticipating the future than in planning its construction. Russia's strategy for 2030 is not formed of abstract musing on what the world might be like then, but of goals and targets and policies to get there. Even these, though, are shaped to some extent by wishful speculations and imaginaries.

Although the volatility of politics, economics and international relations in the early twenty-first century might make us wonder if anything is certain about the future, some things are more certain than others. This chapter's central assertion – that we should not mistake today for forever – builds, for example, on the self-evident fact that people get old and die. For many – perhaps most – observers of Russian affairs over the past decade or so, the terms 'Putin' and 'Russia' are all but synonymous. They are regularly used interchangeably in media reports – 'Putin bombs ISIS', ' Putin sails two warships through the English Channel', 'Vladimir Putin has launched a supersonic missile that could reach the UK in thirteen minutes'. But Putin is not Russia and he will not always be its President. That much is certain, and it is then that the details become speculation. Constitutionally, Russia's Presidents can serve a limit of two *consecutive* terms. If Putin does this by taking the presidency for a fourth time in the election of 2018, and – as he did after his second term as President ended in 2008 – abides by the constitution, he will not be President of Russia after 2024. Whether he engineers a constitutional change, or the positioning of a placeman as during the Medvedev presidency of 2008–2012, is up for conjecture, but whatever the details, at some point Putin's leadership will come to an end.

As certain as the passing of one generation is the rising of another. We cannot know at this distance whether those who rise to power in Russia by the late 2020s and early 2030s will share the values and approaches of the current leadership. We do know, however, that they will have been brought up in a different world from that of Vladimir Putin and his generational cohort. They will be firmly children of the post-Soviet era. In 2014, long-time US scholar of Russia Ellen Mickiewicz published a fascinating book called *No Illusions: The Voices of Russia's Future Leaders* based on detailed focus-group interviews with students at Moscow's élite universities. Of course, one cannot be sure that these students will prove representative of those who come to power in the future; indeed, we noted in Chapter Five the possibility of rising provincial politicians being groomed for pending high positions in the state hierarchy. Nonetheless, Mickiewicz's generalisations avoid the certainty of detail and offer some insight into bright young Russians today. What stands out from her research is the emphasis on how articulate, engaged, strong-minded and individual are her interlocutors. She talks of how knowledgeable they are, most speaking superb English and usually another language or two as well. Nearly all of her focus-group participants have a wide knowledge of the world, from travelling and working abroad and of course from 'living online'. As Mickiewicz concludes, 'they are very different people from the Russian leaders we are used to seeing at international conferences and negotiations'. As for their politics, they are mostly Russian patriots, although that is not the same thing as uncritically supporting the ruling regime. They display, too, dissatisfaction with what the contemporary world has become that they hold in common with rising generations in Europe and America. There is a desire for a democracy that has little to do with comparing the systems of the East and West, and much more to do with wanting an end to corruption, to the abuse of power and to massive wealth inequalities. They see these faults both at home and abroad. In considering the future, a particularly insightful observation arises; the young Russians operate within far shorter time horizons than the American researcher is used to. For her, their short time horizons show that uncertainty plays a central role in the lives of these élite young Russians. Despite the Putin regime's emphasis on stability, and perhaps stemming from their or their parents' memories of the USSR collapsing almost overnight, there remains a sense that – to quote the title, while adjusting the tense, of Alexei Yurchak's superb book on the Soviet collapse – 'everything is forever, until it is no more'.

We can all draw our own conclusions about the validity and relevance of Mickiewicz's by definition narrow focus-group research as regards what it means for the future political leadership of Russia. Less speculative, though, would be conclusions in line with an emphasis that this book has sought from the first chapter to the last, that neither Russia nor the Russians should be constructed in our minds or in our discourses as inexplicably 'other'. People are people the world over, and it is not a matter of surprise – and it is may be even cause for a little mild celebration – that bright students in Moscow's leading universities share the perhaps idealistic desire of their peers in many other countries to reshape the world in a more open, more peaceful and fairer manner.

When we anticipate futures, the most common tool that we reach for is the past. Chapter Eight argued that excessive use of analogies from history can close down our options when considering the present and future. Not every authoritarian leader is a Hitler, but that does not stop the relentless warnings in the United Kingdom against appeasement à la Neville Chamberlain in 1938 every time a foreign strongman throws his weight around on the international stage. The danger of so easy a resort to analogous historical happenings lies in the fact that the details of contemporary situations always differ – and often significantly – from those that prevailed in the previous era. Of more use than precise analogy, when it comes to reading possible futures, is an awareness of long-term historical trends.

One of the few scholars who can be said to have predicted the demise of the Soviet Union was American sociologist Randall Collins, who wrote a book chapter to this effect in the mid-1980s. His prediction was not what is known in the forecasting trade as a 'point forecast', predicting an event to within a year or so of its occurrence. It was more a 'trend forecast', arrived at from his development of a geopolitical theory of state power that looked at long-term patterns and what he saw as their fairly predictable outcomes. Such an approach is not alien to Russian scholars either. The ideas of the Soviet economist Nikolai Kondratiev concerning long-term 'waves', or super-cycles, in global economic affairs have a robust reputation in economics. They have also more recently been applied to contemporary Russian politics. Russian political philosopher Vladimir Pantin, at the renowned Institute of World Economy and International Relations (IMEMO) in Moscow, has written over several years a series of articles on cycles of reform and counter-reform, or liberalism and conservatism, in Russia. Pantin insists on – and extrapolates from detailed analysis of – the connection between these periods in Russian politics and cycles of development in the global economy. In short, such approaches note patterns and repetitions over decades. To oversimplify, but with some degree of confidence, when we look at Russia's future we can do so noting that Russian history over the past few centuries sees waves of international rapprochement and liberalisation swell up before giving way again to more nationalist author-itarianism. Like waves, the respective periods of reform and reaction vary in size and force; nor is the regularity of the shift from one to the other as immutable and predictable as the tide. Nonetheless, the pattern suggests that in the coming decades such policy shifts might come again.

RUSSIA'S FUTURE: AN INSTITUTIONAL APPROACH

This chapter began by considering a relatively common forecast concerning Russia's future –namely, regime collapse – and labelling such predictions as, in most cases, wishful forecasting. It is not so much a matter of considering the collapse of the Putin regime to be somehow impossible or unthinkable – it may happen. It is rather the fact that many such predictions are insufficiently worked out. Credible forecasts require more than jumping straight to an outcome; they require some sense of how that outcome is reached. If the regime is to collapse, by what process will this come about? Will it be a classic revolutionary scenario, where mass demonstrations lead to violent overthrow? Or will some crisis – some precipitous economic decline, some unforeseen natural or technological disaster, some military flare-up or defeat – lead a section of the élite to overthrow the leading cabal? Without a notion of process, forecasts fail to convince.

If we accept that the forecasting of an outcome is incomplete without positing the process that precedes it, then we need to insist too that such a process is based on relatively robust data. Predictions of mass anti-regime demonstrations in Russia of sufficient force to remove that regime from power must at least make some attempt to consider the remarkable popularity of Vladimir Putin; not to mention the regime's hold over the organs of security and violence in the Russian state. Notions of in-fighting among the ruling élite seem a little more likely, but likewise must contend with nearly two decades in which Russia's rulers have been able to shape and control those who sit around or near the political top table.

The point here is not to say that this or that scenario will or will not come to pass. After all, precise political prediction remains beyond the reliable powers of analysts, politicians and lay observers alike. For every prescient display of apparent foreknowledge that is trumpeted as evidence of understanding, there are hundreds of misforecasts that quietly slip away, mistaken and happily forgotten. And of course, we only know which is which once the future has arrived. From the 1990s onwards, the trend in anticipating the future among specialists working in politics and business was to develop multiple scenarios; so far as Russia was concerned, these usually ranged from Western-style democracy to Stalinism reborn. Taking that approach meant that at least one scenario was likely to be celebrated as approximating to the eventual outcome; the rest could be quietly filed away. If the weakness of the scenario approach is its tendency to consider a range of disparate outcomes as equally possible, its strength lies in consideration of the key drivers and frameworks that lie behind the various scenarios.

When it comes then to concluding our consideration of Russia's future path, the emphasis here is not on a range of different outcomes. Even the casual observer can imagine a Russia that is more hard-line than now, or more liberal; more isolationist, or more integrated into global institutions; economically more successful, or in decline. Instead, the focus here is on setting out a potential future for Russia, the path of which can be reasonably marked out from where we are today. To return to this chapter's opening discussion, although the often wishful forecast of radical change remains possible, we might be better advised to dial down the drama and consider rather continuity and incremental shifts; after all, that is what tomorrow turns out to consist of most of the time. What we know about Russian politics is that, since the 1990s, it has displayed a contradictory stability in terms of institutions and leaders. Its constitution and institutional framework remain largely unchanged, and the same people or their chosen successors remain in power. The contradiction lies in the fact that Russia's institutions are democratic in design, while its leadership's grip on political power inhibits serious democratic challenge.

For those whose conception of the current regime's eventual end harks back to the Soviet collapse, the lesson that is too rarely drawn from that process is not that it required a revolutionary toppling of the entire edifice, but rather that the path that the collapse followed was set by the institutional structure in place at the time. Indeed, when the politics shifts, the institutions matter. The Soviet Union broke up because its institutions enabled the republics to secede. Boris Yeltsin's rise to power at the head of an independent Russian state in the early 1990s was enabled by the existence of the Russian Supreme Soviet (or parliament) within the Soviet Union's institutional framework. These institutions, and other key provisions of the Soviet Constitution, had existed for decades, but their formal power had been removed by the ruling regime. Once the grip of the regime had been loosened and political substance given to the institutions' nominal power, the path to regime change was clear.

A similar waking up of democratically dormant power structures awaits Russia's institutions. When looking for a process by which the current Russian regime transforms, or comes to an end, wishful forecasters may be overemphasising revolution and the politics of the street and downplaying the more obvious, more peaceful and more likely institutional route. The institutional framework of Russian politics does not need changing in order for democracy to develop. After all, for the first decade or so of the Russian Federation's existence, the democratic Western states were happy to confirm that Russia's constitution, institutions and indeed elections were fundamentally democratic. The institutions necessary for peaceful regime change in Russia are already in place and accepted by today's ruling regime – nominally at least – as the source of state power. Elections for President and parliament happen on a regular basis, campaigns are organised and opposition candidates agitate for votes. What is required, of course, is the introduction of genuinely free and untainted elections, and – most importantly – that those in power accept defeat when it comes. We are some way from such an outcome, but if we are looking for a process leading to the end of the present ruling regime, the institutional route represents an option too rarely considered.

Today's Russia has become too personalist a political system, with Vladimir Putin assuming a role as 'national leader' that transcends even his formal position as President and head of state. But when, as it surely will, Putin's personalist rule eventually comes to an end, institutions, even previously hollow institutions, will come into their own. Whoever succeeds Putin when he leaves the political stage, even if it is a personally selected appointee, will not have the same standing as 'national leader'. Their power will more clearly lie in their constitutional and institutional position.

The existence of a formally democratic system and process will provide a fresh opportunity for others – possibly from within the ruling regime itself, possibly not – to challenge the successor.

An institutional scenario for Russia's post-Putin path that involves the filling of empty democratic institutions with authentic democratic content sits better with Russia's actually existing polity than do ideas of revolutionary overthrow. As we saw in Chapter Six, President Putin is popular, but his weak spot in the eyes of the Russian people is their perception of the regime's corruption and abuse of power. There is little desire for social and political upheaval, and the Russian people are broadly patriotic and not in favour of movements that might be seen as supporting the West against Russia. Against this background of public opinion, Russia's ruling regime – however emptily – insists that it supports multi-party democracy and despises corruption.

When Putin finally steps down then, the likelihood is that Russia's existing institutions will bear the weight of this pivotal moment. The strong likelihood, too, is that Putin's successor as President will come from within the regime – though perhaps he will be a relatively new face in international terms. The personnel reshuffle at gubernatorial level in 2016 and 2017 (see Chapter Five) suggests that a number of potential replacements are working their way up with the support of the ruling élite. In so presidential a system as Russia, the key questions then centre on any new leader's political position in terms of popularity, patronage and policies. Technocratic competence, demonstrated in running a region – or, in the case of one mooted successor, Anton Vaino, running the presidential administration – has a renewed emphasis among the rising ranks of potential leaders. If that were to be combined with military-security connections and loyalty to the existing regime – as, for example, in the person of the governor of Tula, Alexey Dyumin – then the chances of such a figure becoming President may increase a little more.

As with rising leaders in all political systems, though perhaps more so in authoritarian systems reliant on loyalty and personal connections, the true plans of a new leader are only revealed once they hold power. Mikhail Gorbachev spent decades rising through the Communist Party of the Soviet Union under Khrushchev and Brezhnev, before revealing his dissatisfaction with the very essence of the ruling system once at its pinnacle. As Russian analyst Tatiana Stanovaya has put it, 'the threat to the regime in Russia lies not in revolution but in the emergence of a hidden opposition to the current President inside the élite'. There are those in Russia today who are loyally serving the ruling regime, but would want a renewed, more open and freer system were they in a position to bring that about. Others would prefer a continuation of existing norms. Whichever tendency rises to the top, to quote a well-informed article published by the leading Moscow daily *Moskovskii komsomolets* in 2017, 'if Putin does not occupy a significant post in the regime, the chances of the status quo being retained are altogether close to zero as well. A new broom will inevitably sweep differently.'

Once internal divisions arise, so the hold on power of any given leader or faction diminishes, sources of support are sought, appeals to wider constituencies and the Russian people at large are made and institutions come firmly back into play. Whether by overthrow, or more likely by the formal processes laid down by Russia's constitution and shaped by its institutions, the Putin era is coming to an end within the next decade. We should not mistake today for forever.

SELECTED BIBLIOGRAPHY

For reasons of style, *Inside Russian Politics* does not cite much literature within the text. This annotated bibliography provides details of the few works cited and uses these as a jumping-off point for further reading in several of the genres mentioned.

THINK TANKS

Andrew Monaghan's *The New Politics of Russia: Interpreting Change* (2016), noted in Chapter One, provides an accessible and knowledgeable overview of Russian politics from the primary perspective of international affairs and the breakdown in understanding between the West and Russia. Monaghan has also written or contributed to a number of policy papers for the Royal Institute of International Affairs (also known as Chatham House), notably A 'New Cold War? Abusing History, Misunderstanding Russia' (2015). This and numerous other papers, reports, meeting transcripts and so on are freely available at www.chathamhouse.org in the Russia and Eurasia programme section.

Think tanks of this nature offer excellent sources for considered analysis that bridges the gap between news and academic analysis. As well as Chatham House in the UK, a number of US organisations publish regular material of this nature, including the Carnegie Moscow Center, the Kennan Institute, PONARS Eurasia and the Jamestown Foundation, whose 'Russia in Decline' project is noted in Chapter Nine. For a Russian perspective, as Chapter Nine also notes, the Russian International Affairs Council has an English language website (www.russiancouncil.ru/en/) as does the Valdai Club mentioned in Chapter Seven (www.valdaiclub.com/).

SCHOLARLY TEXTS

Richard Sakwa develops his theory of Russia's political system as a 'dual state' (noted in Chapter Three) in *The Crisis of Russian Democracy: The Dual State, Factionalism and the Medvedev Succession* (2010). Sakwa is the most prolific academic analyst of Russian politics in the West today, having written many textbooks and research monographs, including – in the current decade alone – *Russia Against the Rest: The Post-Cold War Crisis of World Order* (2017), *Frontline Ukraine: Crisis in the Borderlands* (2016), *Putin Redux: Power and Contradiction in Contemporary Russia* (2014) and *Putin and the Oligarch: The Khodorkovsky–Yukos Affair* (2014). He is also one of the editors of the multi-authored textbook *Developments in Russian Politics*, the ninth edition of which is planned for 2018. Sakwa's analysis draws on a deep knowledge of Russia and before that the Soviet Union.

Apart from Sakwa's textbooks, university students studying Russian politics in the United Kingdom and the United States use texts by Eric Shiraev (*Russian Government and Politics*, second edition, 2013), Andrei Tsygankov (*The Strong State in Russia*, 2014) and the volume currently edited by Stephen Wegren (*Putin's Russia*, seventh edition, due in 2018). The author of this book's textbook *Contemporary Russia* (fourth edition due in 2018) offers a wider overview covering Russian politics, society, economics, culture and international relations.

BOOKS BY JOURNALISTS

Mikhail Zygar's book, translated from Russian as *All the Kremlin's Men: Inside the Court of Vladimir Putin* (2016) and noted in Chapter Three, is both representative of a type and unique. It represents the sort of non-academic text that many journalists have written about Russian politics, and as such has a more narrative structure than an academic work, focusing on the 'what happened and who did what' more than on political science theorising.

Examples of such works are many and go back decades – for example, Chapter Nine includes lengthy reference to Anatole Shub's 1969 book *The New Russian Tragedy*. Fine assessments of the Putin years of this type include Peter Conradi's *Who Lost Russia? How the World Entered a New Cold War* (2017), Steven Lee Myers's *The New Tsar: The Rise and Reign of Vladimir Putin* (2015) and Angus Roxburgh's

The Strongman: Vladimir Putin and the Struggle for Russia (2011). Where Zygar's *All the Kremlin's Men* is unique, of course, is that it was written in Russian by an independent-minded Russian journalist with superb access. There is no other English language book that gives an inside story on the Putin regime in this manner, and the fact that it has been a bestseller in Russia demonstrates an openness of political dialogue in contemporary Russia that many Western observers assume to be absent or suppressed.

OFFICIAL REPORTS

Also noted in Chapter Three is Sir Robert Owen's official report on the murder of Alexander Litvinenko in London in 2006 ('The Litvinenko Inquiry: Report into the death of Alexander Litvinenko', 21 January 2016, available at www.litvinenkoinquiry.org). Official reports by Western governmental and related institutions into matters pertaining to Russia have become more common in recent years, and offer interesting – if often contested – insights into contemporary disputes between Russia and the West. As well as the Litvinenko report, 2016 also saw two reports by Richard McLaren for the World Anti-Doping Agency, WADA, into drug use by Russian athletes. In the US the Intelligence Community assessment 'Assessing Russian Activities and Intentions in Recent US Elections' was published on 6 January 2017, and the Defense Intelligence Agency published its 'Russia Military Power: Building a Military to Support Great Power Aspirations' report in July 2017 (www.dia.mil/Military-Power-Publications/).

SELECTED BIBLIOGRAPHY

FROM PUTIN HIMSELF

Vladimir Putin's 'Millennium Manifesto' – the statement that he released when becoming Russia's acting President after the resignation of President Yeltsin on 31 December 1999 – is noted in Chapter Two. It has the formal title 'Russia at the Turn of the Millennium' and was first published on the website of the Russian government. In English it can be found in the appendix to *First Person: An Astonishingly Frank Self Portrait by Russia's President* (2000) by Vladimir Putin with Nataliya Gevorkyan, Natalya Timakova and Andrei Kolesnikov, and translated by Catherine A. Fitzpatrick. An online search will also quickly take you to translations of the document. It is *First Person* that provides the details of Putin's pre-presidential biography and networks set out in Chapter Three. The official statements, speeches and diary of Russia's President can be followed day-to-day on the English language version of the presidential website at www.en.kremlin.ru/. Key speeches to look for here or more widely online include the annual addresses of the President to Russia's parliament, and – as noted in Chapter Eight – Putin's speech to the Munich Conference on Security Policy in 2007, and his speech welcoming Crimea into the Russian Federation in March 2014.

FICTION AND MEMOIR

Sophia Creswell's novel *Sam Golod* (1996) is the source of a quote used in Chapter Two because it encapsulates so well something of the mood of the early 1990s in Russia. Creswell's novel is one example of several English authors who turned their experience of life in the extraordinary world of post-Soviet Russia into literature. In *Sam Golod*, Creswell not only captures the chaotic combination of hardship, despair and excitement of those years beautifully, but she – or rather her central character, the young English teacher Natalie – does this with the awareness that, as a Westerner, she could throw herself into this world with an immunity that comes from being able to leave it at will and return to the secure comforts of the West.

A similar thread runs through the wonderful novel *Snowdrops* by A. D. Miller, shortlisted for the Man Booker Prize in 2011, which again draws on personal experience of the 'Wild East' that was Russia after the Soviet collapse to tell the story of an English corporate lawyer caught up in the social and economic whirlwind of post-Soviet Russia. Other English writers with experience of life in Russia chose memoir rather than fiction as their genre. Susan Richards followed up her excellent insight into Russia at the time of the Soviet collapse, *Epics of Everyday Life* (1991), almost two decades later with *Lost and Found in Russia* (2010). Tig Hague wrote a highly revealing memoir of an involuntary couple of years spent in Putin's Russia, incarcerated in its prison system (*The English Prisoner*, also known as *Zone 22*, 2009).

In several places in *Inside Russian Politics* mention is made of Russian fiction. *Zavtrak s poloniem* (*Polonium for Breakfast*) noted in Chapter Three has not been translated into English, a situation common to the vast majority of thrillers and crime novels to be found in Russia's bookshops. There are hundreds of these and they tend to draw on themes such as organised crime, oligarchs, Russia's military interventions and so on. Chapter Nine, however, notes a number of Russian novels set in the future that are available in English, such as Dmitry Bykov's *Living Souls* (2011), Vladimir Sorokin's *Day of the Oprichnik* (2011) and Dmitry Glukhovsky's series *Metro 2033* (2010), *Metro 2034* (2014) and *Metro 2035* (2016). Other novels by Sorokin and Glukhovsky have been translated into English, as have works by leading Russian authors such as Olga Slavnikova (notably *2017: A Novel*, published in English in 2012), Ludmila Ulitskaya (*The Big Green Tent*, 2015) and Zakhar Prilepin (*Sin*, 2014).

INDEX